"The Banker's Secret to Permanent Family Wealth"

John Cummuta

john@smartestwealthsystems.com

Live your life...

And build your wealth...

Using the SAME money

Preface

Hi, I'm John Cummuta, author of

- *The SMART Wealth System™* Course
- *Transforming Debt into Wealth*® System
- The *Debt-FREE & Prosperous Living*® Basic Course
- *Are You Being Seduced into Debt?*
- *Wealth Machine: How to Start, Build, and Market a Debt-Free Business That Fits Your Life*
- *The Power of Perpetual Income*
- The *Wealth Generator System™*
- *The Credit Solution*
- *Debt-Elimination 101*
- The *Customer-Focused Direct Marketing* book
- The *SMART™* direct marketing system
- The *Sales Machine™* database marketing system
- Co-developer of the *DebtFree™ for Windows*® debt-elimination software

All these publications led to my being invited to teach my *Transforming Debt into Wealth*® seminar at 13 Tony Robbins *Wealth Mastery*® events around the world.

I list all these publications simply to show that I didn't just decide yesterday that teaching personal finances would be a good idea for a book. I've been teaching personal finance strategies and systems for more than 25 years.

Almost everything I've written and taught has been to help my fellow middle-class Americans and their children survive an increasingly slanted personal-finance playing field.

Stagnant incomes, increasing debt loads, Social Security system weakness, dwindling pension plans, stock market risks, and the banking industry's money-siphoning siege against our personal wealth has stacked the deck against hard-working Americans.

The result: this faithful group is left with insufficient resources to achieve anything like financial independence.

It's been my mission for 2½ decades to offer people an exit ramp from this financial system that is steeped in seduction and manipulation, designed to suck the financial life out of them during their income-producing years, and then spit them out when they're older.

At the point in life when they need to be enjoying the fruits of their labors, they find the tree bare, because it's been stripped along the way by those they thought were their financial allies.

Through all my books, courses, videos, audios, software, and seminars, I've been privileged to help more than 3 million people worldwide get on track to a much better financial outcome than they were headed for by default.

I'm truly humbled by that, but the reason I've written this book is that, in the last few years, I've learned and implemented a powerful *new* method to develop financial freedom, that builds on what I've taught in the past and supercharges it.

This book, *The Banker's Secret to Permanent Family Wealth*™, represents this latest evolution.

What I taught in my previous publications was correct, in terms of the deceit of debt and its insidious consequences.

Published by SMARTEST Wealth Systems – © Copyright 2017 • John Cummuta • all rights reserved

However, my wealth-building concepts were conventional, in a time when convention was becoming increasingly dangerous.

I sought out and learned the concept I reveal in this book after experiencing the stock market's 2000 and 2008 crashes. I know many people who thought they were going to retire in those years, who were forced to continue working... some until this very day...some until they died.

These hard-working friends and family trusted "the system," by saving in qualified plans, which were invested in the stock market. I call this the "Chuck and Hope" plan, where you *chuck* money into your 401k and *hope* it will be there when you'll eventually need it.

I wish it worked as hoped, but the research is clear. These plans are NOT helping people sufficiently prepare to ever completely stop working. There is a better way.

The financial tool revealed in this book is a real alternative to qualified plans and other savings vehicles. It's a cash accumulation and deployment platform that consistently and safely grows your money, without stock market risks, while simultaneously letting you use your money for any reason at any time without restriction.

This remarkable mechanism not only provides a safer, more dependable money-growth account, but it is a superior device for overcoming many of the other financial challenges we face.

For example, you can use this system to pay off your debts, buy cars, fund college educations, build a business, invest, and more, while building your wealth – <u>with the same dollars at the same time</u>. Want to know how that's possible? Turn the page.

Contents

Introduction – How You Gonna Get There?

Everybody wants to achieve "financial independence." However, that phrase has different meanings to different people.

I think it's more precise to say that we all want to enjoy financial stability now, and then hit retirement age – whatever that means to us – with enough dependable income to continue living a rewarding lifestyle, until we join our ancestors.

However, very few people are on a trajectory that will get them there. In fact, the vast majority of people are headed for a never-ending work-life, or at least a seriously diminished lifestyle in their "golden years."

Please stop your brain train for a moment and ponder that.

If you're just bopping along, living like most of the people around you, carrying a typical debt load, and spending money like most of your friends and family do, you're probably not managing your finances in a way that will work out like you're hoping it will.

I'll explain the research proving this point a little later in the book.

You need a plan

If you're not following a plan designed to get you to a <u>specific financial outcome at a specific time</u>, you are likely fooling yourself as to how well your financial life will play out.

Do you have a plan?

Have you ever defined your post-employment lifestyle with any specificity – like *when* you want it to begin, *where* you want to live, *what* you want an average day to include, *how much* monthly income it would require, and so on?

Face it – **the answers to these questions should be driving your daily financial choices and decisions**.

If you haven't clearly defined these targets, your subconscious mind – which does most of the problem-solving work in your life – is left to assume targets from your closest friends' and family's goals, from cultural and family history models, and from your own unspoken conclusions.

Here's the critical point about this: your subconscious mind will work tirelessly to get you to the destination you give it...or the one you leave it to assume.

Whatever that destination turns out to be, **you will live in it for a long time.**

Statistics show the average person will live 2 decades or more past traditional retirement age. We *hope* these decades will be our most enjoyable, but we can be almost certain they'll be our least energetic and physically capable, so shouldn't we be planning to be a bit easier on ourselves during those 20+ years?

Wouldn't it be good if those decades were the least financially taxing years of our lives?

Seems reasonable, yet most people live with a stunning disregard for planning their 4th quarter finances. They consume their incomes during their peak earning years, and then eek out an existence for their last 2-3 decades.

And then we see them in their 70's, handing out food samples at Sam's Club, collecting shopping carts at Target, or asking, "Do you want fries with that?"

Most people don't give enough thought to how much it will cost to live comfortably when they no longer want to work full time. They put their future financial requirements last behind their current indulgences, their lifestyle competition with friends and family, and their kids' futures.

My heart breaks to see so many good people living post-employment lives far below their working lives, and way below their hopes and dreams of decades earlier.

How bad is it?

Since I don't know your personal situation, I'll use national statistics to paint most people's reality. For objective data, I'll turn to the Employee Benefit Research Institute's latest report on *Individual Retirement Account Plans*.

The below figures show how much the average person has in savings by age grouping.

- < 35: $6,306

- 35 – 44: $22,460

- 45 – 54: $43,797

- 55 – 64: $69,127

- 65 – 75: $56,212

- 75+: (sample size insufficient)

OK, let's put these figures into perspective.

Financial Planners will suggest you limit your retirement withdrawals to about 4% of your nest egg each year. At a 4% withdrawal rate, your nest egg should last as long as you do.

To find out how much you need to have in retirement savings for this withdrawal rate, divide the amount of gross income you'll need each year in retirement by 0.04 and you'll have your target nest egg amount. For example, a $50,000 annual gross income would require a nest egg of $50,000/.04 or $1.25 million.

Look at the above savings by age groupings again. Do you see an average savings amount anywhere near $1.25 million?

But you'll be getting Social Security, right?

OK, let's assume you'll collect the average Social Security income of $1,229 a month. That would add up to $14,748 a year, leaving $35,252 a year to be provided by your savings and investments. At a 4% withdrawal rate, your nest egg would now have to total $881,300.

Again, average Americans aren't saving anywhere near that much.

There's no hope!

Are you feeling a little behind the power curve, considering these figures? Understandable.

Published by SMARTEST Wealth Systems – © Copyright 2017 • John Cummuta • all rights reserved

Then, let's look at common methods to save up your $881,300.

48,691
40P

- **Investing.**
  OK, I'll need to assume an age here, so I'll go with the middle of the above age ranges. That would be about 55. I'll also assume you already have the average $69,127 in your savings or portfolio by that age. What will it take for you to grow that amount to $881,300 in a decade?
  - o Let's be optimistic and say you could invest $1,000 a month for the next 10 years. You would need to find an investment that would return an average 32.6% each year to get you to the $881,300 you'll need by retirement.
  - o Good luck finding that rate of return. According to research firm Dalbar, Inc. the average long-term stock market mutual fund investor gains just 5.19% annual ROI.
- **A business of your own.**
  An additional income stream can make a big difference to both your current and long-term financial pictures, but for right now, we'll assume you're a regular income earner, so we're only talking about your ability to save and invest from your paycheck.
- **The lottery.**
  Since you have a statistically better chance of being struck by lightning than of winning the lottery, you may as well jump on every email chain letter and Facebook post share that promises wealth if you forward it to your whole list. I'd also eat a lot of Chinese food to up your chances of scoring a great fortune cookie promise.

Doesn't look like you can win, does it? Of course, you could do a "Kirk, Kobayashi Maru" maneuver.

If you're not a *Star Trek*® fan, I'll explain.

James T. Kirk is the only Star Fleet Academy cadet to beat the Kobayashi Maru test. This is a test of how a starship commander would deal with a no-win situation, much like you may face in terms of building up anything like $881,300.

So how did Kirk beat the test?

[handwritten: └ 620,761 - GSP]

He reprogrammed the training simulator so he could win. In his own words, he "Changed the conditions of the test."

Similarly, you can change many of the conditions of your life by the time you reach your post-employment years.

In these pages, I'm going to show you how to have *more* money at your disposal during your working years...and money you can withdraw, as a retirement income supplement, when you would like working at a job to be optional for you.

We call it "Job-Optional Income."

To achieve this goal you'll have to really want it, because it's your level of desire that will determine your likelihood of success.

The principles I'll show you will work 100% of the time.

Will you?

Published by SMARTEST Wealth Systems – © Copyright 2017 • John Cummuta • all rights reserved

What's Your *Why*?

Your *why* is the answer to the question, "*Why* would I undertake the discipline and effort necessary to achieve this or any other financial game plan?"

Your *why* is your overarching, gut-level, emotional purpose for making and saving more money, both in the short and long term. So, what are the factors that make up your *why*?

Is your *why* to buy your life back?

I have a friend who's a chiropractor. He invested 8 years of training and $150,000 of tuition to become one, and he's a good one. But after more than a decade in business he realized that his practice owned him, not the other way around.

His *why* was to buy back his time. He didn't want to achieve financial independence just so he could ride around in a fancy car and live in a nice house. He was already doing that. He wanted to not have to be constantly thinking about or managing his practice.

Even though he had other chiropractors and necessary support staff working in his practice, they just *worked* there. He was the owner, so he had to worry about bringing in new patients, paying the $40,000 monthly overhead, and keeping up with the latest equipment and technology.

He was thinking about it all the time. He wanted a life beyond the business. That was his *why*.

What's yours?

I know single parents who desperately want to raise their own children instead of paying daycare workers to do it. That's their *why*.

I know parents who would give anything to make it to all their child's little league games, or better yet coach the team. That's their *why*.

I know many people who just want to stop worrying if one of their utilities will be shut off this is the month, because they're always behind with the bill payment. That's their *why*.

What's yours?

- Are you half way or better to retirement age with nowhere near half of what you'll need to retire?
- Are you hoping to be able to help a child or grandchild get a great education?
- Would a vacation home or just a better home make life a lot more enjoyable?
- Would it be deeply rewarding to be able to give people money instead of just well-wishes when they tell you their very real troubles?
- Would you like to give more at church or to important charities?

What is your *why*?

You need to find the answer inside you; probably deep inside, if you want to connect with your most motivating *why*.

Some things are obvious in the *why* department, like healing the scars of an underprivileged childhood, or easing financial stresses on a relationship, or closing other emotional wounds that could be alleviated by achieving financial security.

These are powerful *why's,* and they're more impactful if they're consciously focused on.

In other words, it's worth the time to dig deep for your most emotional why's. Then capture them on paper, on your computer or other device, and post them where you'll regularly see them, to remind your subconscious mind *why* you need to stay on course.

Your why's are your persistence fuel. They will keep you on the wagon in those times when you'd just as soon roll off.

They may feel like your worst enemies or ghosts that are haunting you, but they are your best friends, and you'll celebrate with them someday.

Now, if you're thinking any of this is optional for you...

Published by SMARTEST Wealth Systems – © Copyright 2017 • John Cummuta • all rights reserved

Chapter 1 – This Is No Drill!

Here's what *Forbes* Magazine columnist Edward Siedle recently said in a *MoneyNews* article.

"The United States is failing to prepare but is nonetheless set to witness the world's greatest retirement crisis. People are living longer, but there are growing indications that many can't afford to live comfortably in their golden years.

"Findings from the Employee Benefit Research Institute (EBRI) reiterate the harsh reality reported in other surveys: Americans do not have enough money to retire.

"According to EBRI, more than half of U.S. households possess less than $25,000 in savings and investments when their homes and pensions are excluded from the picture. Many have no pension to consider in the first place, as the trend of extending these benefits is evaporating. And those that are so lucky to receive them better watch out. If an unexpected need for $2,000 arose in the next month, only half of U.S. households could find the money.

"Whether you know it or not someone is busy trying to figure out how to screw you out of your pension,"

Siedle considers 401(k)s, which were marketed as placing people's futures in their own hands, as a great experimental disaster. He was once employed as mutual fund legal counsel, and says the way retirement funds were sold to working Americans is "almost laughable — if the results were not so tragic."

As we are already seeing, many older people have had to return to work because they either could not afford the costs of living or they need employer-subsidized healthcare. Others realize they need more money so they work longer, considering themselves to be postponing retirement. But many Americans have put ideas of retirement aside and plan to work as much as they can for as long as they can.

In the end, most people will end up in the same boat, according to Siedle, "with deteriorating health, a lack of employment opportunities and insufficient funds...too frail to work, too poor to retire."

Scary...and completely true

People who intended to stop working over the past decade, and those who hope to stop working in the future, face nearly impossible odds.

As I think back to when I started my journey as a financial educator, I'm stunned by the differences between then and now. It was so much simpler at the beginning of the 1990's. Since then, we've watched the stock market crash twice and the government spiral into indescribable debt.

These two changes impact you and me in two ways:

1. Almost all qualified plans – 401(k), 403(b), IRA, SIMPLE, Keogh, etc. – invest your contributions in the stock market. A stock market, as I'll shortly show you, which cannot be depended on to grow your savings.
2. Taxes in qualified plans are *deferred* not eliminated. So, if your savings in these accounts do happen to grow, you'll eventually pay taxes...**on the higher amount** rather than the amount you're deferring the taxes on now. In other words, your taxes are growing with your portfolio.

This means that money you have in qualified retirement accounts is vulnerable to the heartless, undependable temperament of the stock market, and its growth is earmarked to cover the spending frenzies of an out-of-control government.

When the rubber meets the road, governments have just one source of money to feed their voracious fiscal appetites, and that's from their citizens.

So here we sit, between the stock and the hard place... between the markets and the government.

The stock market, like Las Vegas, let's you win now and then to keep you in the game; but eventually the house always wins. And whether you win or lose in the markets, you're still going to owe the deferred taxes.

Run for the Exits

I know a lot about markets and how they work, and I'm completely out of both the stock and bond markets. When I fully understood the system that I explain in this book, I moved all my 401k money to an IRA, and then liquidated the IRA as fast as I could move the money into this new system.

Yes, I paid the taxes. It was worth it to me to get off the stock market roller coaster. Besides, I was going to pay the same or higher taxes later.

Fortunately, I was over 59 ½, so I didn't have the penalty to consider, but the bigger issue was that I did not want to risk a 2000 or 2008 crash <u>right when I planned to start using the money</u>.

Stock markets can't be trusted with any money you can't afford to lose.

One of the smartest stock market professionals I know, a guy who was a big shot with a large national brokerage firm and who publishes a highly-regarded stock trading advisory service, spends most of his time and energy building a network marketing downline. That's how unreliable the market is. Those who know the most about it don't keep all their eggs in that basket.

The same goes for bond markets. Even though they have an aura of safety, nothing could be farther from the truth. While the interest (coupon) from a bond is generally guaranteed, the face value is not unless you own it personally and hold it to maturity.

If you own bonds through a mutual fund, when interest rates go up, you could lose your shorts, elastic band and all.

Investing is not the same as Saving

Published by SMARTEST Wealth Systems – © Copyright 2017 • John Cummuta • all rights reserved

"Saving," and "Investing," used to mean different things. People *saved* up for retirement, and if they had some mad money beyond that, they'd do a little "speculating" in the markets.

Stock market investing was largely a game for the rich; but in the 1970's, the government blurred the distinction by creating qualified "retirement" accounts, like the 401(k).

These accounts were almost exclusively vehicles for investing in the stock market, a game most working people had no experience in. However, the accounts were promoted like retirement *savings* accounts, so a lot of people bought in...and put their future in the hands of the Wall Street gamblers.

Putting money into paper securities is like laying it down on a Las Vegas green felt tabletop. You should only use money you can afford to let the spinning wheel or cards take away from you, without damaging your life.

The market's not safe...and it's not that productive

I've spent more than 25 years showing people all around the world how to pay off their debts as rapidly as possible. Debt-elimination has been my primary mantra and goal for the millions of people I've taught through the years.

But deep down I've known that – as important as debt-freedom is – it is only half the financial-freedom formula.

You also need a system to turn your former debt payments into wealth. Such a system must include both a secure place to keep your wealth and a dependable, safe system to grow your wealth.

The stock market is not such a place or system.

The below chart speaks for itself. It shows the U.S. stock market's total return over time. While it occasionally peaks, it then takes back everything it gave you. And if you break the chart into decades, you'll find very few that generously rewarded investors.

S&P 500 Rolling 10-Year Average Annual Total Return as of 12/31/2011

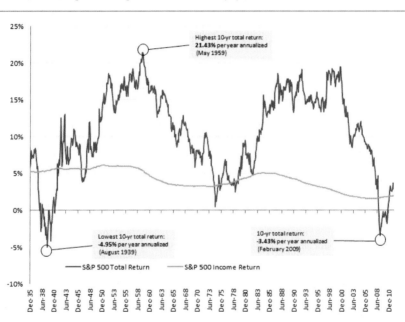

Source: Blackhorse Analytics; S&P

Most produced moderate growth or terrifying losses.

Dalbar Inc. is a company which studies investor behavior and analyzes investor market returns. The results of their research show that **the average equity mutual fund investor – for the last 20 years – earned a market return of only 5.19%.** And that's before taxes.

That number may have you scratching your head.

If it sounds low to you, that could be because the market may have been stronger recently. We tend to evaluate most things in our lives by our most recent experiences. But our short-term market view is deceptive when compared to a longer window of 10-20 years.

Why is the average investor's return on investment so low?

Because, the typical investor gets nervous when the market declines, yet they try to hang on. If it turns out to be a serious correction or bear market, their patience runs out near the bottom and they sell at a much lower price than they bought in at (sell low). They conclude it's better to be out of the market than to endure such losses.

When the market starts recovering, this inexperienced and now-burned investor doesn't trust it. So, they sit on the sidelines watching institutions and experienced individual investors jump in.

Finally, after the market has proven to them that it really is going up, they jump back in somewhere near the top (buy high), just before the next correction or downturn.

Most people are not experienced enough, nor do they have the temperament, to successfully manage market swings, so they lose. They feed their money to brokers, mutual funds, and more savvy investors.

I'm actually a little surprised they end up averaging a positive 5.19%.

The stock market has proven lethal to millions of would-be retirees, yet most financial advisors and teachers have been

Published by SMARTEST Wealth Systems – © Copyright 2017 • John Cummuta • all rights reserved

telling their followers to, "max out your retirement accounts, dollar cost average, and stay in the market."

I, on the other hand, have grown increasingly silent over that time about how to build wealth, because I wasn't sure myself! I was sure back in 1991, but since 2000, it's been a different reality.

Here's what changed...

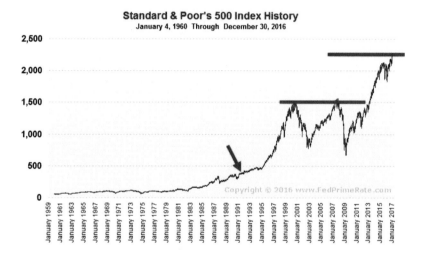

Standard & Poor's 500 Index History
January 4, 1960 Through December 30, 2016

When I first started teaching my debt elimination concepts in 1991 (red arrow), I was telling my students that – once they were debt free – they should pack their newly-recovered monthly cash flow into qualified retirement accounts and invest those funds in the stock market through mutual funds.

That was good advice...for the following 9 years. Then, in 2000 the "Tech Bubble" popped, and the market proceeded to lose half its value. However, for someone who had started investing in 1999, **it lost all its value!**

Yet, the pundits were saying that buy-and-hold was still alive, and if we just hang in there, Mister Market would come back and reward our steadfastness.

Well, Mister Market did come back beginning in 2003, and it looked like the pundits were right...until 2008 when the floor fell out again because the real estate bubble popped.

OK...fool me once, shame on you. Fool me twice, shame on me. I was through believing the pundits.

Can you afford to lose a decade?

Someone who started investing in the stock market in 1999 was **back to even** a decade later. Those ten years produced two surges and two crashes that brought them right back to where they started. If we factor in inflation, they were still behind.

The market took their money. The mutual fund managers took their fees. The brokerage company took their fees. And the investor ended up with nothing.

A lost decade!

Can you afford to lose a decade of saving for your future? How about if it's the last decade right before you plan to stop working?

Major market corrections (30%+) happen every 7-8 years, on average. Twenty+ percent corrections happen an average of every 3.5 years. How long has it been since the last one?

The Middle-Class Trifecta

In addition to market risks, the average American is being crushed by interest costs and the taxman.

We've discussed market risks, and most folks know about the taxman's bite, but we're often less aware of the severe toll that interest costs levy against our wealth.

Thirty-four and a half percent of the average income-earner's take-home pay is spent on interest charges.

It saddens me when I see people crowing about improving their investment returns by 1% or 2%, while they're coughing up 30+% of their after-tax income to interest. On their mortgage alone most people are paying an effective interest rate over 85%, because they're in the first decade of their latest mortgage!

Just check your monthly payment coupon or your loan amortization schedule to see how much of each monthly mortgage payment is interest.

In this book, I propose to solve all three problems for you:

1. I'll show you a saving/investing system that will give you good, dependable growth that will never go down. You will **never** lose any of your retirement funds because the market decides to "correct."
2. This system will **protect your money from taxes**, from judgments (varies by state), and from government avarice. Your money will grow tax-free, you'll be able to use it tax-

free, and the government can't take it to pay their overdue bills.

3. This system will allow you to **recapture the money** you're currently losing to interest...and all that interest will earn interest for you!

After years of my closely watching the system explained in this book, it has proven itself to check all the important boxes.

- ✓ It must be as **safe** as, or safer than, a CD or bank savings account.
- ✓ It must offer real **growth** potential – guaranteed.
- ✓ It must offer **access to** all my money, if necessary, without penalties or restrictions.
- ✓ It must **protect** me from taxes.
- ✓ It must **not require a dramatic lifestyle change**.
- ✓ It must **complete** its wealth-building mission for my family even if I die before accomplishing it myself.
- ✓ It must give me a way to build wealth **with the same money** I use to make purchases or even pay off my debts!

I wish I would've started sooner!

In the early 2000's people began asking me to check out this unique financial concept. I considered it and found it fascinating, but it was sufficiently outside my box that I didn't want to begin trumpeting its benefits without more examination.

At that time, I was running around the world teaching seminars with Tony Robbins, and I had a best-selling course being advertised on radio across the country.

So, for the next 10+ years I let this concept sit on the back burner. Then I did a look-back comparison of its results versus all the typical markets we invest in – stocks, bonds, and real estate – and started kicking myself around the house for not starting on this path myself 10 years earlier!

I now I feel so strongly about its advantages over traditional wealth-building options that I am compelled to share it with you. I'm convinced it should be the bedrock of nearly everyone's personal finances.

I feel so much better about this system than I do about the stock market or any other typical investing market that I have moved most of my, and my wife's, liquid assets into this vehicle. I can't tell *you* what to do, but I can tell you what *I'm* doing...where my conviction is today.

I sincerely believe that not using this system leaves you exposed to unnecessary financial risk, and it leaves you throwing potentially hundreds of thousands of interest-dollars down the drain as well.

It's called a Private Family Bank

The Private Family Bank™ is based on the same principles bankers use to get and stay wealthy.

Smart businesspeople will set aside millions of dollars in capital, go through a multi-year qualification process for a bank charter, and then invest more millions to build bank buildings and advertise for customers

Why?

Because they know they will thereafter make mountains of money, and they'll do it without using a penny of their own cash after the front door opens!

I now recognize the Private Family Bank™ concept as the answer to my search for a dependable family wealth-building system to replace volatile and dangerous markets.

More than that, it's a way to make that family wealth-building system permanent, so that succeeding generations can become wealthier and wealthier instead of dissipating the money as is usually the case.

Let's begin our exploration of the Private Family Bank™ with the problems it solves.

Chapter 2 – Beat the System by Becoming the System

You're being robbed!

More than half the money you earn is being stripped out of your life, most of it involuntarily, but a lot of it with your active consent.

Look at where your gross income goes:

- 28% of the average American's gross income goes to income and payroll taxes.
- 25% goes to interest payments. (34.5% of after-tax income)
- 42% goes to living expenses.
- 5% goes to saving and giving

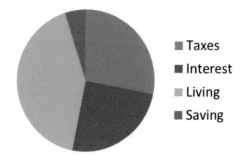

Obviously, if you're like most people, it's impossible to build financial independence with **less than half** your income – especially in undependable investment markets.

According to the Employee Benefits Research Institute:

- 64% of 65-year-olds have **less than $50,000 saved**.
- Yet, 65-year-old men can expect to live an average of 17 years beyond 65, and women an average of 19 years.

- A 65-year-old couple has 50% chance of needing $450,000 above Medicare for medical expenses.

If most 65-year-olds don't even have $50,000 saved, how do they expect to pay their expenses for nearly 2 decades after retirement age? That would break down to about $4,000 a year to live on, in addition to whatever they'll get from Social Security and perhaps a pension.

And, if they can't afford a robust Medicare supplement insurance policy, they'll be broke as soon as any big medical bills hit. They'll have to liquidate all their assets, fall into poverty, and apply for Medicaid.

Of course, those are savers. Investors must be doing better, right?

Well, they are doing somewhat better. According to a Fidelity Investments quarterly analysis, the average 401(k) account reached **a record $92,500** in 2016, but that's a drop in the bucket compared to what a household will need to live nearly 2 decades after retiring – especially if they end up in the 50% that will require medical funds beyond what Medicare provides.

So, whether they're saving or investing, the data is clear. People aren't saving or investing enough. Why not? Because of where this chapter started: they're being robbed! **You're** being robbed!

Taxes and interest sweep away more than half the average American household's gross income. And then, when the next correction comes along, the stock market often steals what they've managed to squeeze out for saving.

In other words, it seems like an impossible dream to save and grow sufficient wealth to live an enjoyable post-employment life.

But what if you could...

- **Keep the 34.5% of your *after-tax* income** lost to interest payments?
- Have all that interest earn interest itself?
- Enjoy Guaranteed growth – no recessions or corrections?
- Reduce your taxes and your heirs' taxes?
- Pay off your cars, home, student loans, credit cards, while **simultaneously** building retirement wealth...**using the same dollars**?
- Dramatically reduce investment risk?
- Eliminate contribution and withdrawal restrictions of typical retirement plans?
- Enjoy unrestricted liquidity, control, and use of your money for *any* reason?
- **Protect your wealth** from creditors, judgments, and law suits?
- Build your wealth **tax-free**?
- Be assured your wealth plan would succeed even if you are disabled?
- Be assured your wealth plan would succeed even if you die before you complete it?
- Withdraw your wealth **tax-free**?
- Transfer your wealth to your heirs **tax-free**?

Published by SMARTEST Wealth Systems – © Copyright 2017 • John Cummuta • all rights reserved

That would change things

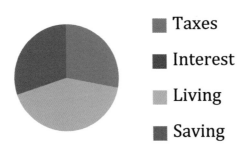

- Taxes
- Interest
- Living
- Saving

30 % would go to saving and giving, instead of just 5%.

And some of the 42% going to living expenses could pay off your debts and build your wealth...**at the same time**!

How can you build such a system?

You need to change who profits from the use of your money. You need to change who controls the use of your money. In other words, you need to change boxes!

What am I talking about?

Banks, brokerage firms, insurance companies, and other financial institutions are just boxes in the money pool. They each have their label and their sign over the door, but they're just boxes that money flows into and out of.

We get hung up on the labels, but the people who own and run these institutions don't.

For example, if a large developer approaches a bank for a loan to build a big apartment complex – but the bank doesn't have sufficient resources of their own to cover the loan – they might borrow a block of money at a low interest rate from an insurance company, and then lend the money to the developer at a higher interest rate.

As far as the developer knows, he or she got the money from the bank. Meanwhile, the bank sits in the middle, grinning, and making the spread between the 2 interest rates, with none of their own money in the game.

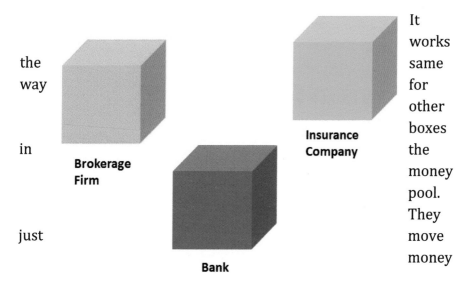

the way in just

Brokerage Firm

Bank

Insurance Company

It works same for other boxes the money pool. They move money among themselves as needed. They recognize each other as functional boxes in the money pool, and they operate in concert to put their money to work profitably.

So, what does this mean for you and me?

It means something a lot more exciting than just a way to squeeze another percent or two out of our investments. It means that if you and I just change boxes, we can effectively **become our own bank!**

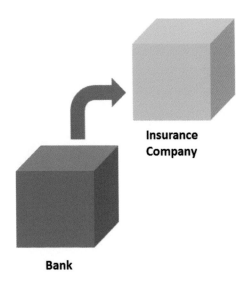

Insurance Company

Bank

Your Private Family Bank™

If you're willing to disregard the labels over the doors, I'll show you a way you can start using the insurance box to become your own bank.

But first let's look at why this is a good idea.

How banks make money

Banks make money by being middlemen in our financial transactions.

You deposit money in your savings account, and the bank pays you a whopping ¼% to ½% interest. If you deposit a large amount of money, say $50,000, they may be generous and give you 1% to 2% interest!

So where does the bank get this ¼% to 2% to pay you?

If someone needs a mortgage, the bank will lend them money deposited by you and other depositors, charge borrowers 5% or more interest, and give you ¼% to 2% of it.

If someone needs to finance a car, the bank – either directly or through the dealership finance department – will lend depositor money to the borrower at 6%–8% or more (even on cars they claim offer 0% interest).

If someone uses a credit card, the bank is lending them depositor money and charging them 12% or higher interest.

Published by SMARTEST Wealth Systems – © Copyright 2017 • John Cummuta • all rights reserved

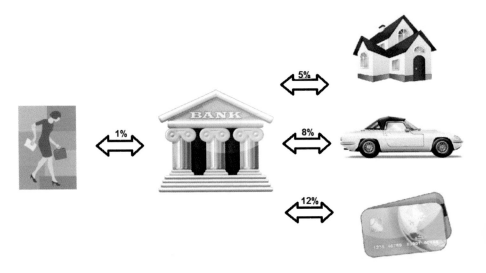

So, the bank, with no skin in the game, makes a spread of 4%, 7%, 11%, and more! Pretty good return for them...on your money! No wonder businesspeople are willing to go through so much time and paperwork to start or even buy a bank.

It's a money machine!

On the other hand, if you're the borrower in this picture, your interest payments represent money forever lost from your life. It is building the bank owners' wealth.

You are the bank's investment.

It's helpful to remember that every dollar that comes into your life is going to build *someone's* wealth, and you get to decide whose. The best way to keep this money in your life and have it build your wealth is to become the bank owner.

That's exactly what I'm going to show you how to do, but first let's see how that would change the traditional bank picture. How would the numbers look if you were the depositor, the borrower, **and the bank**?

How your *Private Family Bank™* makes money

The images are the same, but the interest being paid by the borrowers (you and your family) now belongs to you, the bank owner. It goes into your bank and earns compounding interest for you.

You were going to be paying that interest to someone anyway, so making the payments to your bank doesn't change your lifestyle or cash flow…just your ultimate wealth.

And look at what happens to the measly ¼% to 1% a traditional bank was paying you on your deposits. The money you deposit in *your* Private Family Bank will pay you up to **20 times as much!**

It's better to be your own bank, don't you agree?

Published by SMARTEST Wealth Systems – © Copyright 2017 • John Cummuta • all rights reserved

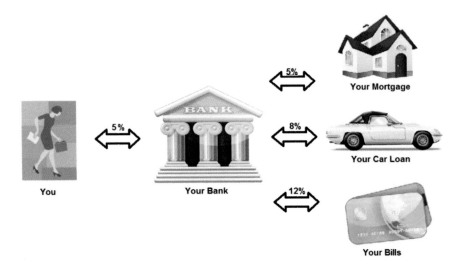

When you want to take out a loan from your own bank, for any reason, it won't require an application, credit check, proof of income, or anything else to qualify for the loan. In effect, you'll just ask yourself (the bank owner) for a loan, and you (the bank owner) will say, "Yes!"

In most cases, it will be as simple as logging into your policy online, typing in the amount you want, and clicking the submit button.

If you take a loan from your Private Family Bank™ and – for any reason – you can't make a loan repayment for one or more months, you just don't. Missing a loan payment won't affect your credit score, and it won't block your ability to get additional money from your bank.

The only consequence of missing a payment is that the unpaid interest for each missed month will be added to the loan balance. But, since a typical Private Family Bank™ loan interest rate is 5% annually, each month's interest is only 0.4% (1/12th of 5%).

Forget the box labels

You make deposits into your bank, and you withdraw money through checks, debit cards, ATMs, and loans.

You make contributions to your brokerage account, 401(k), or IRA accounts, and you withdraw that money through distributions or loans.

You make premium payments to your life insurance company, and – if you have the right kind of policy – you can take money out tax-free through the policy loan facility or withdrawals.

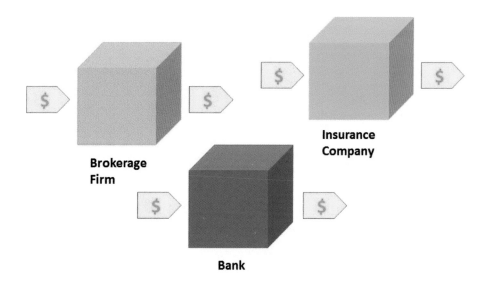

It's all just money in – money out.

The labels on the boxes or on the types of deposits and withdrawals are not important. However, the difference in whose wealth that money is building is crucial.

Here's why changing boxes can be so powerful for you

The below chart shows a typical American household's use of their after-tax income.

Thirty-four and a half percent goes to interest (yellow segments). The red part of each bar shows the principal amount: the money you borrowed for your cars, homes, and consumer items.

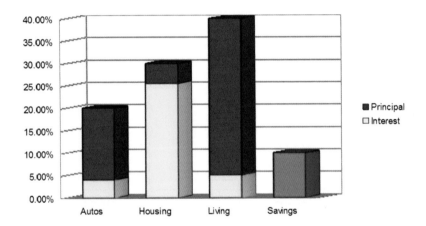

Interest is the most damaging enemy of your personal financial success. Interest payments on personal (non-business) purchases have no redeeming value, even if they're tax-deductible.

You will earn a finite amount of money in your life. Sending a major share of that money to banks as interest payments, instead of saving it, is the most common reason people end up far short of what they need for retirement, educating their children, covering medical expenses, traveling, and just enjoying their golden years.

Published by SMARTEST Wealth Systems – © Copyright 2017 • John Cummuta • all rights reserved

Over a lifetime, the compounded interest you won't earn on that money can be staggering.

Here's interest compounding *against* you over time

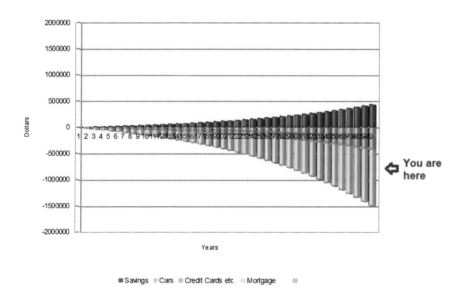

This chart shows you sending interest to traditional banks, on your credit card purchases, car purchases, home mortgage and equity line of credit, student loans, etc., where it compounds for them. These are huge, wealth-draining losses for you.

But, if you are the bank, you could flip this chart over.

The 34.5%, or whatever percentage of your take-home pay is going to interest charges, also represents **your greatest financial opportunity**.

If you can redirect this large chunk of money back into your own interest-earning account, it can literally change your financial life.

We hear the "change your life" thing a lot, but this rerouting of interest that you're already paying truly can have that kind of impact.

When interest becomes savings inside *your* bank

With a Private Family Bank™, instead of just saving 5% 10% of your take-home income, you could be saving nearly 45%!

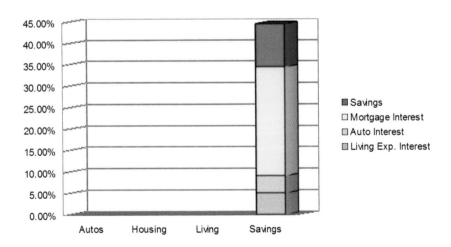

With your own bank, the majority of interest paid on your cars, home, and consumer purchases will stay in your financial system, and thereby add to your savings.

This could change what would otherwise be an expense – lost interest money – into an investment. What most people consider just a cost of being a consumer (interest charges) could turn their lives around and give them a real chance at financial security and an enjoyable post-employment life.

The power of this system cannot be overstated.

It can make the difference between enjoying retirement and just surviving retirement. It can make the difference between your children and grandchildren enriching traditional bankers when they pay back their student loans or enriching you...and potentially themselves, depending on how you have it set up.

Sounds good, doesn't it?

Let's make that interest compound *for* you over time

It has been widely reported that Albert Einstein was asked what he considered to be the most powerful thing in the universe, and without hesitation he said, "Compound interest."

Whether the story is precisely true, the answer is arguably accurate, because the compounding effect causes interest you earn today to earn interest itself tomorrow. Interest is growing on top of itself and multiplying. It gets bigger and bigger at a faster and faster rate.

No wonder geniuses are impressed by it.

But those of us who are not geniuses often lose sight of the steady, unrelenting power of compounding. In this give-it-to-me-right-now culture, we're not well equipped to wait for compound interest to do its work. It feels like watching paint dry.

However, when we do exercise patience, compounding is impressive! All it needs is some amount to start with.

So, how about starting by rerouting the pile of interest most of us are paying out to our creditors? It is more than enough for compounding's power to make us wealthy – very wealthy.

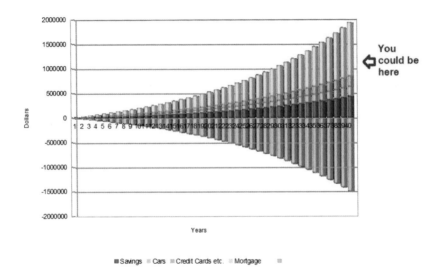

In the simple example chart above, the difference in outcomes between interest charges being paid to outside banks (compound interest working *against* you) and those charges being paid into your bank (compound interest working *for* you) is almost $3.5 million!

Which curve would you rather be on – the lower poverty curve of you sending your wealth to traditional banks as interest charges, or the upper wealth curve, where that money is going to your bank and building your wealth?

That's what I thought.

If this Private Family Bank™ thing is starting to sound good to you,

Then what you want to do is...

Chapter 3 – Open Your Own Private Family Bank™

It's as simple as 1, 2, 3

1. Start your bank
2. Capitalize your bank
3. Use your bank

1. Start your bank

To be clear, we are not starting an actual bank. We are using the financing facility of a whole life insurance contract to *function* like a bank for us. I'll discuss *why* whole life versus term life later.

Ironically, this is the **same financial instrument** that banks use to invest their tier one capital for guaranteed safety and growth. They call it BOLI or Bank Owned Life Insurance. It is owned by most banks and recommended by the FDIC.

One banker was quoted in the book, *Pirates of Manhattan.,* saying, "It's our bank's best performing asset."

If it's a *bank's* best-performing asset, perhaps it should be *our* best-performing asset.

We won't call it BOLI, because you and I are not technically banks, but we will use the same concept and the same instrument – dividend-paying whole life insurance – to achieve the same ends: safety, liquidity, and growth.

A Private Family Bank™ is NOT an off-the-shelf, generic whole life insurance policy.

To maximize its banking capabilities, you need a **specially-designed** life insurance contract with a mutual (policyholder-owned) life insurance company. Not all life insurance companies are "mutually owned."

You won't likely hear about this kind of policy from your friendly neighborhood insurance agent for 2 reasons:

1. Most insurance companies do not offer this kind of policy contract, so their agents could not build one for you, even if they knew how.
2. This policy structure reduces the agent's commission by 50% to 70%, because it's designed to maximize your cash accumulation rather than your death benefit, and an agent's commission comes primarily from the whole life policy's death benefit provision.

Most life insurance agents have never even heard of this concept, because their management never tells them about it. Why not? Because of the commission reduction.

We at SMARTEST Wealth Systems, on the other hand, are willing to give up 50% to 70% of the potential commission to help you start your Private Family Bank™, because our primary mission is financial education.

I only got my first insurance license, because my students couldn't find agents who knew how to build a banking policy or who were willing to take the commission cut. Today, I and my team are licensed across the country, so we can help you start your Private Family Bank™ no matter where in America you live.

2. Capitalize your bank

Where will you get the money to start and grow your bank?

Are you saving any money now? Are you contributing to a 401(k) or IRA each month? Do you have an emergency fund in a savings account or CD?

If you answered yes to any of these questions, I'd argue that your Private Family Bank™ can prove a better destination for some of that money. It could be safer and more productive as premium dollars going into your banking policy than into other accounts.

I'm not saying you should cash out of your qualified plans to capitalize a Private Family Bank™. However, you could consider whether some of your current savings contributions – into qualified plans and elsewhere – might be better utilized as premium dollars capitalizing a Private Family Bank™ of your own.

What about my employer match?

If your employer is giving you an immediate dollar-for-dollar match for your contributions into your 401(k), you should probably keep funding it to the extent your contributions are matched, but anything above that amount could be rerouted into premium dollars for your Private Family Bank™.

Dollars going into a Private Family Bank™ are not going away. They are simply going from one account you own into another account you own, and are available to use anytime you need them – with none of a qualified plan's restrictions.

Published by SMARTEST Wealth Systems – © Copyright 2017 • John Cummuta • all rights reserved

Money in IRS qualified plans is wrapped in chicken wire. You can shove money in through the holes, but it's extremely difficult to get any money out – especially if you're younger than 59½.

In addition to excess retirement plan contributions, another place to look for Private Family Bank™ premium dollars is any money you have going into savings accounts.

How about my debt-elimination money?

Are you overpaying bills to get out of debt sooner?

I understand debt elimination. That's my specialty. However, I've come to appreciate how a Private Family Banking™ policy can be an even more powerful platform through which to pay off your debts than simply overpaying your creditors.

So, I'd suggest rerouting debt overpayment dollars to premium dollars. Paying off your debts *through* your Private Family Bank™ results in more wealth than just paying off the same debts directly to your creditors.

Every dollar you're using to eliminate your debts remains in your bank earning interest and dividends at the same time it's paying off your debts.

At the end of the process, your debts are paid off AND all the dollars you used to do it are still in your bank, continuing to grow.

So, I recommend you at least consider redirecting debt overpayment money into your own bank as premium dollars. Then take money out of your bank to pay off your debts. I'll explain how a bit later.

This won't hurt.

If you're currently saving money or contributing to a qualified retirement plan, you're used to that money going into those accounts right now. And, if you're overpaying bills to reduce debt balances, you're also used to that money being unavailable for spending.

So, using these dollars for premiums to capitalize your bank would not change your current lifestyle. They would, however, dramatically improve your future lifestyle.

Can we find more premium dollars?

Beware of the CIA

We humans tend to waste a lot of money on **C**onvenience, **I**ndulgence, and **A**ppearance.

So, once you've identified premium dollars you can appropriate from money you're already sending to savings or debt elimination, the next layer would be looking for money you are unnecessarily spending on things for which there are easy, less expensive alternatives.

For example, a designer coffee and a muffin ($7-$10) on the way to work each day can easily add up to $150-$200 a month. Going out to lunch at fast-food eateries each workday can add another $150-$200 a month. Premium cable or satellite channels add up, as do visits to the sports bar or Friday evening hangout.

You probably enjoy these treats, but are they more important to you than financial independence?

Published by SMARTEST Wealth Systems – © Copyright 2017 • John Cummuta • all rights reserved

In the appendix of this book I've included a *Premium Finder Form* you can use to chase down dollars that are leaking out of your life like this. Dollars which could be put to better use capitalizing your Private Family Bank™.

Premium Finder short list:

- Your current income
- Money already in savings accounts, as well as ongoing savings deposits
- Qualified retirement plan contributions beyond employer match, or for which you believe a Private Family Bank™ would be a safer destination.
- Cash value in other life insurance policies you own
- Money freed up by debt consolidation
- Money currently used to overpay monthly debt payments
- Money wasted on Convenience, Indulgence, and Appearance

Premiums can be paid annually, semi-annually, quarterly, or monthly, and can include additional lump sums.

Premiums can be designed to accommodate extra contributions during the year. We call it "headroom."

Note: you cannot rollover a qualified plan (401k, IRA, etc.) into a Private Family Bank™ policy. The IRS only allows rolling cash value from an existing life insurance policy – that you own – into a new Private Family Bank™ policy. Doing this starts your new bank off with cash value that the insurance company can immediately begin paying you interest on.

So, how much do I need for premiums?

Because your Private Family Bank™ will be built on a whole life insurance contract, there are some structural considerations, as well as minimums set by the insurance company, which result in a practical minimum premium of about $300 a month.

Above $300, a good next tier number is a $417 per month premium. That adds up to a nice, round $5,000 a year.

Does $417 a month sound like a lot? Well, the typical month contains 176 working hours. That would equate to $2.37 an hour. Is your financial future worth $2.37 an hour? Of course, it is.

However, the more important reason to think in these dollar terms is that they will allow your Private Family Bank™ to start accumulating a useful amount of money. When you put $5,000 a year into a Private Family Bank™, within the first year there would be enough in your bank to pay off a credit card or two.

You want to put as much as you can into your bank's premiums, because **you're trying to build wealth**. Think in terms of how much accumulated money would be impactful in your income-earning years, as well as how much you'll need to have accumulated to have a beneficial impact on your post-employment finances.

If the purpose of this strategy is to build a pool of money you can use to pay off your debts, and take over financing major purchases, and to build up a nest egg you can retire on, then be as aggressive as possible funding it.

Published by SMARTEST Wealth Systems – © Copyright 2017 • John Cummuta • all rights reserved

I have clients who contribute $300 a month up to clients building their bank at multiple thousands of dollars a month.

Start where you are. **We can always open additional Private Family Banking™ policies for you as your debts are paid off or your income increases.**

START is the most important word in wealth-building.

3. Use your bank

If you just take steps 1 and 2, start your bank and capitalize your bank, it will perform as a safe and profitable investment like a savings account or CD, and it will grow faster than any bank saving vehicle. It could even outperform the stock market over time, because it will never experience a loss.

However, if you also take step 3 and use your bank as a bank...

Your cash value can grow even faster. How?

Simple: you will be paying the interest you're currently sending to other banks to your bank instead. No rocket science. It's just a redirection of your cash flow.

You'll do this by paying for major purchases with policy loans from your Private Family Bank™ rather than with credit cards, auto loans, and store financing. But policy loans are not free...

Published by SMARTEST Wealth Systems – © Copyright 2017 • John Cummuta • all rights reserved

Policy loans charge interest

The insurance company we most often use charges 5% interest on loans.

You might be asking yourself, why would I pay interest to use my bank's money? Two reasons:

1. Accessing your Private Family Bank's cash value through the loan facility avoids potential taxes on interest and dividends in your bank.
2. The insurance company charges a relatively low interest rate, so the math works in your favor.

Since all the money you put into your bank stays in your bank earning interest and dividends, growth is being calculated on an **ever-increasing amount. So, interest and dividends are also ever-increasing.** See the green line in the below graph.

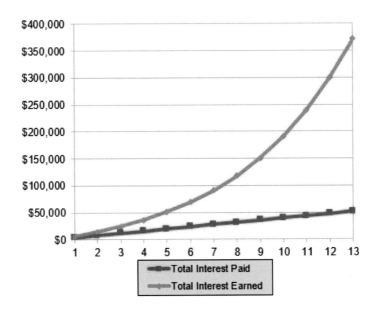

The 5% being charged on a loan, on the other hand, is being calculated on a continually-decreasing balance, as you reduce it with your loan repayments. See the red line in the graph.

The result: **your bank's cash value is always far outgrowing your loan costs**.

Once people get this "secret sauce" benefit of their Private Family Bank™ they look for every opportunity to put more money into their cash value.

The above graph is based on a series of car loans, every 5 years, over a lifetime. I'll use a specific car purchase example in a few pages. You'll find it very interesting.

This is different, isn't it?

Unfortunately, most people never have a life insurance contract explained to them as a living financing system, because most insurance agents look at whole life insurance as a death benefit with a nice little savings account inside.

However, in the real world, most people have a much greater need for finance than they do for a death benefit.

The way a Private Family Banking™ policy is constructed – maximizing its financing benefits while you're still alive – it becomes a good savings/financing/investing account with a nice little death benefit inside.

You get to be the recipient of the borrower's interest payments, and those interest payments grow in your cash value, earning interest and dividends from the insurance company!

You can use your bank to...

Finance the things of life:

- Cars
- Homes
- College educations

And invest in other wealth-building assets:

- Real estate
- Precious metals
- Oil and gas

Let's buy a car

There are 2 common ways to buy a car:

- Borrow from *a* bank
- Pay cash

You could lease a car, but that's such a financially horrible exercise I won't even deal with it here. If you borrow money to buy a car, at least you end up with an old car. Leasing is just long-term renting. Lots of money leaves your life, and you're left with "poof!" nothing. Let's stick with buying a car.

Most people finance their car purchases. A few people, who have a better grasp of the onerous cost of interest, save up for their cars and pay cash. The borrowers know they're paying interest. However, the cash buyers – who think they're avoiding an interest cost – are paying interest also.

Borrow from a bank

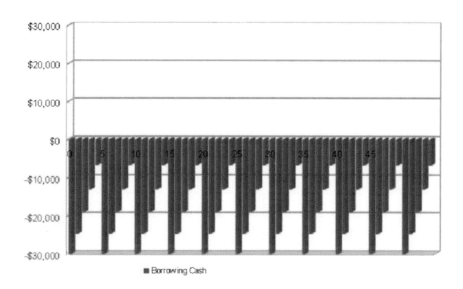

The borrower in our example above goes to the bank for $30,000 to buy their car. Over the next 5 years they gradually pay the loan back with interest, finally decreasing their debt to zero.

About that time, however, they decide they need a new car. So off to the bank (or the banks' representative in the dealer's financing office) they go. Back in the hole for $30,000, they begin the long hard trudge paying their loan back to zero.

Since the borrower is paying the price of the car plus interest, they will pay more for the car than the cash buyer will.

Now let's pay cash

In the below chart, the cash buyer (blue bars) saves up the money to pay cash for the car, so it takes – in this example – the same 5 years. Once he or she has the $30,000 saved up they liquidate the account and go buy their car.

Their savings account falls to zero and, if they're smart, they immediately begin saving for their next car purchase. If they don't, they will eventually have to be the borrower and get the money for their next car from the bank.

Paying cash

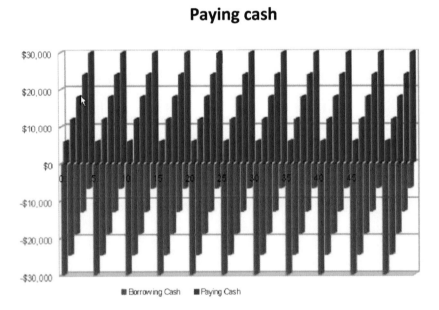

Which is better?

Well, let's look at the chart. Notice that both the borrower and the cash buyer are continuously racing up and down to zero. And **they're both paying interest!**

The borrower pays the obvious interest charged on their loan for the car. The cash buyer, on the other hand, is "paying" the cost of the interest they will no longer earn on the money they liquidated out of their savings account to pay cash for their car.

This lost interest for the cash buyer seems like an unavoidable cost of buying things the right way, the cash way. I mean, how else can you do it?

Could you expect to be able to take the $30,000 out of your savings account but continue earning interest on that $30,000?

Not in a regular bank. But in a Private Family Bank™ you could! We'll see how that works in a moment.

For right now, just understand that, if you use a traditional bank to finance or even save up for your car purchases, the bank wins either way. The following chart shows us how much the bank profits as the middleman in these transactions.

Using a traditional bank

	A	B	C	D	E	F
1	Cost of Purchase	Interest Rate	Frequency of Purchase			
2	$30,000	5.5%	5			
3						
4	After		11 purchases			
5						
6	The Borrower has spent			-$378,203		
7						
8						
9	The Cash Buyer has spent			-$330,000		
10						
11						
12	Do you want to know how much the bank has made?					
13						
14				$380,820		
15						

In this example, both buyers make a car purchase every 5 years, and they do it 11 times over their car-buying lifetime.

The cash buyer pays 11 times the $30,000 purchase price, for a total of $330,000. The borrower does indeed pay more than the cash buyer: $48,203 more in interest charges over the 11 car purchases.

But look at the big red oval. The bank made $380,820 – which is more than either of the two car buyers ran through the bank.

Even more remarkable is the fact that the bank used **none** of its own money. They lent the cash buyer's $330,000 to the borrower, and then paid a small fraction of the interest the borrower paid them to the cash buyer as interest on their savings account.

The bank had no skin in the game but made a third of a million dollars!

It pays to be the bank.

Since long before Jesus threw the moneychangers out of the temple, bankers have been making a fortune on the spread between the price they pay depositors for money and what they charge borrowers for that same money.

Let's see how much better it would work for you if you were the bank.

We'll buy those cars again, only we'll finance the purchases through your Private Family Bank™.

Published by SMARTEST Wealth Systems – © Copyright 2017 • John Cummuta • all rights reserved

Financing through *your* Private Family Bank™

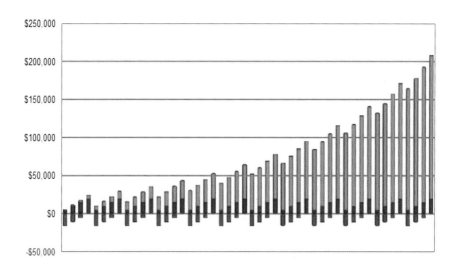

The small red and blue bars on the above chart are compressed versions of the borrower and cash buyer from the previous chart, and the green bars represent your money growing in your bank (your policy's cash value), because you're financing your own car purchases.

It starts as small earnings on the money you're saving for your first car purchase, but instead of the account dropping to zero with the first car purchase, as it did when the cash-buyer took their money out of a savings account to buy each car, **the full capital, the interest, and dividends stay in your bank and continue earning interest and dividends.**

Instead of making payments plus interest to an outside bank, you can choose to make those same payments – at the same interest rate an outside bank would've charged – back into your own bank, recapturing what would have been lost money, so it can also earn interest and dividends in your cash value as well.

Over time, the cash value growth (green bars) accelerates, and while you just go about saving up and buying cars every 5 years, your wealth builds in your bank to more than $380,000!

Remember, you are doing nothing more than the cash buyer did in our original example. You're just saving up for your $30,000 car and then withdrawing that amount to make each car purchase.

The difference – that builds up to more than $380,000 of real, cash wealth for you – is the compounding of interest and dividends paid into your growing cash value in your Private Family Bank™.

There's no difference in how much you're sending to the bank each month, compared to what you would have sent to a traditional bank.

But there is a difference in where those payments are going.

They're going to your Private Family Bank™, so your cash flow and lifestyle are unaffected. Only your wealth is affected... and very positively!

As I mentioned earlier, the insurance company we use in most states is currently charging 5% interest on policy loans, so how could you pay your bank 21% interest?

There is a way we can make room in your banking policy for interest you want to pay beyond the 5%. Let's see how Tom and Mary did it.

Published by SMARTEST Wealth Systems – © Copyright 2017 • John Cummuta • all rights reserved

Tom and Mary's PFB

Tom and Mary decide to start a Private Family Bank™ to buy cars and to eventually supplement their retirement income, so from age 31-34 they pay $10,000 a year in premiums.

That's only 4 years of premiums for a total of $40,000.

A year later they begin buying cars with policy loans, purchasing a new one every 5 years, as in our previous example.

Tom and Mary are honest bankers, so they repay the loans to their bank. However, they decide to pay a higher interest rate than the 5% their insurance company charges on all loans.

The additional (above 5%) interest they pay is $333 a month. That adds up to the policy's approximate $4,000 annual base (minimum) premium. So, they're still making premium payments, but they're doing it with the extra loan interest dollars on their car payments.

This means they're paying the same total monthly amount they would likely be paying had they financed the car with an outside lender, but it is split in 2 parts and is going to the insurance company through 2 doors: the loan repayment door and the premium door.

Tom and Mary are using car payments – something they would be doing anyway – to put more cash value into their policy, and they're increasing the policy's death benefit at the same time.

And then comes retirement

At age 70, they start taking $30,000 a year out of their Private Family Bank™ to supplement their retirement funds. They have no intention of paying this money back, and the insurance company is fine with that.

By age 85 they've taken $743,458 out of their bank in loans for cars along the way and supplemental income in retirement.

Yet, even after taking out nearly three quarters of a million dollars in car loans and retirement funds, Tom and Mary still have $26,876 in available cash value in their bank! And they still have a $162,237 remaining death benefit.

That's so good, I have to summarize it.

Tom and Mary's Private Family Bank™ performance:

- $743,458 generated for cars and living expenses.
- $26,876 remaining cash value.
- $162,237 remaining death benefit above cash value.
- **$932,571 total value to their family.**
- They only put in $40,000 in initial premiums, plus $136,187 of ongoing base premiums, which they viewed as additional interest on their car loan payments.

Here's where the magic is

Tom and Mary financed their car purchases with policy loans (right side of the below illustration). These loans were collateralized by their ever-growing cash value (left side of the dashed line), but the loans never reduced that cash value.

Then Tom and Mary overpaid the insurance company's required interest rate by an amount (blue curved arrow) that would pay their base (minimum) premium. This continued to grow their bank's cash value.

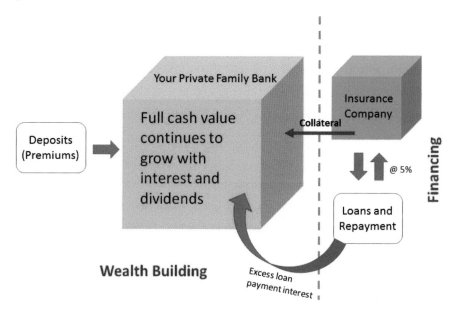

You can do the same thing

As I explained earlier, you may be paying a third or more of your after-tax income to outside banks as the interest component of bill payments.

Recapturing that interest is the biggest potential gain available to you with this system, because not only does the interest end up in your bank instead of someone else's, it earns interest and dividends itself. It compounds!

You just saw how Tom and Mary overpaid their car loan interest to build their cash value. How about if I told you I knew where you could add 17% to your cash value, would you be interested?

Well, look no further than the plastic rectangles in your wallet or purse, because, according to CardHub, the average interest rate paid on credit card balances by people with fair credit is 21%.

So, if you make those same purchases with money from your Private Family Bank™ and pay your bank the same monthly payment you would've paid to your credit card banks, **you become a guaranteed 17% return investment for yourself!**

That's the difference between the 21% interest rate the average credit card would charge you and the 5% loan interest the insurance company would charge you.

To grow your cash value in this example, you would pay your bank 21% on credit card purchases, 5% of which would be paid as loan repayment and 17% as additional premium, just like Tom and Mary did with their car payments.

In practical terms, you would use your credit card to make the purchase, and when the credit card bill came, you would borrow the money from your Private Family Bank™ to pay off the charge on the card, and make your 21% payments to your bank.

What about Tom and Mary's unpaid retirement loans?

When you start taking supplemental income from your Private Family Bank™ in your post-employment years, that's

Published by SMARTEST Wealth Systems – © Copyright 2017 • John Cummuta • all rights reserved

called an "Income Stream." This money will come to you tax-free, so you can spend 100 pennies out of every dollar.

When you first begin income stream withdrawals, the insurance company sends you money from the premium dollars you paid them through the years. Since you paid your premiums with after-tax dollars, there is no tax due on this money.

When all your premiums have been returned to you, and you would begin receiving interest that the insurance company added into your cash value, they seamlessly switch you to policy loans, so the money will continue coming to you tax-free.

If you die with an outstanding loan balance, the insurance company will pay the balance off from your death benefit. The remainder of the death benefit will then go to your named beneficiary(ies).

Important: if you take a max loan, and don't make any repayments, you risk the accruing unpaid interest growing to an amount that could lapse the policy, causing it to be cancelled. But rest assured, the insurance company would be sending you many reminders to start putting the policy back into balance before that would happen.

Pay off debts through your Private Family Bank™

The below chart is called a "Headwind Analysis." This is a real case study.

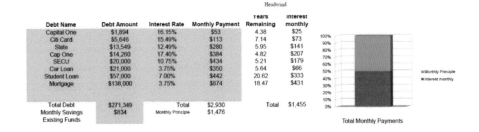

Debt Name	Debt Amount	Interest Rate	Monthly Payment	Years Remaining	Interest monthly
Capital One	$1,894	16.15%	$53	4.38	$25
Citi Card	$5,646	15.49%	$113	7.14	$73
Slate	$13,549	12.49%	$280	5.95	$141
Cap One	$14,260	17.40%	$384	4.82	$207
SECU	$20,000	10.75%	$434	5.21	$179
Car Loan	$21,000	3.75%	$350	5.64	$66
Student Loan	$57,000	7.00%	$442	20.62	$333
Mortgage	$138,000	3.75%	$874	18.47	$431
Total Debt	$271,349	Total	$2,930	Total	$1,455
Monthly Savings	$834	Monthly Principle	$1,476		
Existing Funds					

Total Monthly Payments

See the red section of the bar graph on the right? That's the portion of this family's total monthly debt payments that is lost to interest…every month.

Almost half!

Most people pay their debts each month thinking that a small fraction of their total monthly payments is going to interest – certainly no more than the interest rate of the highest-interest debt.

The reality, however, is that most middle-class Americans are paying about half of their total monthly debt payments to interest, some a little less, some a bit more, but it's almost always right around half.

The good news is that this is also the amount this family can gradually recapture and reroute back into their Private Family Bank™, meaning **they can eventually be building wealth with this $1,455 a month.**

Here's the result of their Private Family Bank™ debt elimination process:

- They started with **$271,349 total debt**, including credit cards, a student loan (20-yr amortization), a credit union loan, a car loan, and a home mortgage (just under 20 years left).

- **All non-mortgage debts are paid off in 6 years.**
- **The mortgage is paid off less than 2 years later**
- **Saving them $81,776 in interest charges.**
- By the end of the year in which their debts are paid off, there will be **$55, 325 in their Private Family Bank™**.
- **And they've freed up $35,165 a year** in former debt payments that they could use to start another Private Family Bank™!
- If the husband dies before the debt payoff plan is completed, **their "loved ones' bank" (the death benefit) pays everything off immediately!**

This is better than paying off the same debts directly

If you accelerate paying off your debts by making additional principal payments (overpaying) directly to your creditors,

- You will free up the monthly cash flow you had been wasting on debt payments.
- You will become the true owner of the assets and property on which you had been sharing ownership with the bank.
- And you will save yourself more than $80,000 in interest charges you'll never have to pay in the future.

However, all the money you used to pay down your debt balances will reside with your creditors.

On the other hand, if you pay your debts off through your Private Family Bank™, you will enjoy all 3 of the above debt-elimination benefits…AND…**the money you used to pay off the debt balances will still be in your bank earning interest and dividends.**

How we pay off debts through a Private Family Bank™

You'll need to prime your bank with capital before starting the debt-elimination process. That can be done by paying annual premiums, or with a lump sum added to or including your first-year premium, or with a gradual cash value build-up through monthly premiums.

This priming allows interest and dividends in your bank to begin creating the growing wealth curve shown in our earlier car-buying example.

If you pay your debts off directly to your creditors, you send additional principal (money beyond the required payments) to your creditors monthly. When you pay off debts through your Private Family Bank, on the other hand, you wait until your policy's Available Loan Amount is enough to completely pay off your smallest-balance debt.

Here's how the process works

Your Available Loan Amount is the portion of your policy's cash value that is available to use as collateral for a policy loan. When you have no outstanding loans, your Available Loan Amount is generally about 95% of your policy's cash value.

When you take a loan, thereby using that much of your collateral, that correspondingly reduces your Available Loan Amount. However, as you make loan repayments, the amount of each payment is immediately released from collateral, and is part of your Available Loan Amount again.

When your Available Loan Amount is enough to completely pay off your first debt, you take a policy loan for that amount and pay it off. Then simply redirect the monthly payment amount you had been sending that creditor to the insurance company as a monthly loan repayment.

Notice that this hasn't changed your cash flow, because you're sending out the same amount you were before.

However, it has begun accelerating your debt payoff timeline, because you're sending the insurance company a repayment amount that was calculated at the higher interest rate of the debt you paid off with your policy loan. This larger payment amount will pay off the balance faster than if you just sent the insurance company payments calculated at 5%.

Now, start watching your Available Loan Amount again, and when it's enough to completely pay off the next smallest-balance debt, take a policy loan for that amount, and completely pay off the debt. Then ADD its former monthly payment to the payment from the previous debt that you've been sending to the insurance company as loan repayment.

From there, you simply rinse and repeat your way through all your debts.

All through this process, your Available Loan Amount will be increasing at an accelerated rate, because both your regular premiums and your growing loan repayment amount will be simultaneously increasing it.

Another method to accomplish the same debt-elimination outcome is to take maximum-available loans annually, and completely pay off as many debts as you can – from lowest balance to higher balances.

If there's anything left from the policy loan, after you've paid off the debts you can completely pay off, apply it to the next debt in the lower-to-higher-balance sequence. Then this debt's balance will be that much lower when you take out the max-available debt-elimination loan next year.

Just repeat this annual process until all your debts are paid-in-full.

I like the method of paying off individual debts as soon as my Allowable Loan Amount is sufficient, because I am able to pay off debts throughout the year, thereby gaining a sense of momentum. The outcome of both systems will be pretty much the same.

Back to our debt-elimination case study

Below is a spreadsheet showing, year by year, how the debt elimination process unfolds for the debts listed in our Headwind Analysis above.

The burgundy bars show how long it would take to pay off individual debts without the Private Family Bank™ acceleration process.

Published by SMARTEST Wealth Systems – © Copyright 2017 • John Cummuta • all rights reserved

The much shorter green bars show how quickly each debt will be paid off by using a Private Family Bank™ to do it.

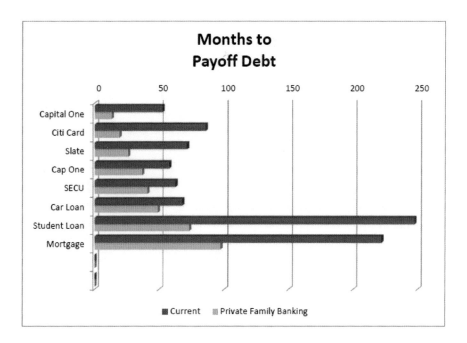

Each time a debt is paid off, its recaptured monthly payment is added to the loan repayment amount these folks are sending to the insurance company.

This is where repayment acceleration is happening.

You can see the time acceleration in the above graph.. But how much money are they saving?

The below graph shows how this family will save $81,776 in future interest charges they'll never have to pay, if they follow their Private Family Bank™ debt-elimination plan.

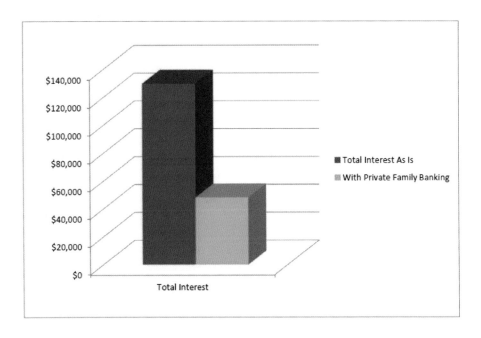

It can work this way for you too

It may take several months or more to capitalize your bank sufficiently to pay off your first debt, but you'll be simultaneously building wealth as you pay off your debts, because your debt-elimination dollars never really leave your cash value. They're always in there, earning interest and dividends, as long as you live.

We at SMARTEST Wealth Systems would be happy to work out a debt-elimination plan for you with your specific numbers. Just email info@smartestwealthsystems.com or call 602-527-3969 to start the conversation.

It should be clear by now that a Private Family Bank™ is a wealth-growing vehicle by itself, and it can be supercharged when you use it as a bank to finance current purchases or to pay off past purchases, especially if you pay your bank back at a higher interest rate like outside financing sources would charge you.

Let's invest *through* your PFB

Another way to supercharge the total return from your Private Family Bank™ is to use it as a platform for investing.

If you're going to invest, where will the money come from to make each investment? It will almost always come from cash you've accumulated in a bank account or cash in a brokerage account.

What if you store your cash in your Private Family Bank™ in between investments instead?

As with debt elimination, when you use money from your bank to fund an investment, those dollars remain in your bank's cash value earning interest and dividends at the same time they're earning whatever return your outside investment generates.

The below spreadsheet shows a $100,000 investment. It's a loan to a business that is building a bakery, and the borrower promises to pay the loan back over 7 years (84 months) at an annual interest rate of 12%. So, they will pay the investor 84 monthly payments of $1,765, totaling $148,283.

These numbers are shown above the burgundy bar on the spreadsheet.

Not bad. That's a $48,283 profit! Whoops...isn't that the taxman over there. Yep, and he wants 20% of your gain, reducing it to $38,626. But that's still a solid 39% return on investment.

To make this investment, most people would have to pull the $100,000 out of savings, thereby losing the interest it had been earning. So, their only gain would be the $38,626.

But let's say you're making this investment from your Private Family Bank™. This is shown below the burgundy bar.

Investment	Number of Monthly Payments	Loan Interest Rate	Monthly Payments	Total Re-Payment	Gain After Taxes	Percent Gain	Tax Rate
$100,000	84	12.00%	$1,765	$148,283	$38,626	39%	20%

Using Policy		Policy Loan Rate	Monthly Re-Payments	Total Re-Paid to Policy			
$100,000	84	5.00%	$1,413	$118,725			

		Extra Interest	Monthly Taxable Gain	Total Taxable Gain			
		7.00%	$352	$29,558			

Starting Cash Value of Policy	Number of Months Invested	Earnings Rate of Policy	After Tax Gain Added Monthly	Future Cash Value of Cash Policy	Percent Gain	Advantage of Policy
$100,000	84	5.00%	$282	$170,047	70%	81%

This will be a policy loan, so you won't owe any taxes. And as I said earlier, the insurance company won't take the $100,000 from your policy's cash value to lend it to you. Instead, they'll use $100,000 of your cash value as collateral for a direct loan from the insurance company's general fund.

So, your $100,000 is still earning interest and dividends inside your Private Family Bank™...at the same time you're lending it to the bakery company.

The insurance company only charges you 5% interest on this loan, while the investment is paying you 12%.

This is one of those opportunities to overpay interest, to accelerate your cash value growth. So, instead of just paying the $1,413 monthly payment to the insurance company that would cover 5% interest, you will overpay the interest as additional premium payments, which will build your cash value.

The investment pays you $1,765, but the insurance company only charges you $1,413. That leaves an extra $352 a month!

Whoops isn't that the taxman again? Yep. He wants $70 a month from your $352 monthly profit, leaving $282 after taxes. This small tax exposure is the only piece of this process the tax man has access to, because it happens outside your Private Family Bank™. But let's not focus on the $70 of tax. Let's follow the $282.

You put that $282 into your policy's Paid Up Additions rider, commonly called PUA's. PUA's are effectively a pipeline into your policy's cash value, which is your bank. PUA's buy a bit of additional death benefit, but most of the money goes right into your cash value, where it begins earning interest and dividends.

Meanwhile, the $100,000 that never left your cash value in the first place, is still in there earning interest and dividends as well.

The result is that, over 84 months, including both the internal gain on the $100,000 and the $282 you're feeding into Paid Up Additions, your cash value will grow to $170,047!

That's a $70,047 gain, which is a 70% return on investment, and because it's inside your Private Family Bank™ this gain is tax free!

Published by SMARTEST Wealth Systems – © Copyright 2017 • John Cummuta • all rights reserved

That sure beats the 39% after-tax return from the investment done outside a Private Family Bank™. And, to be fair, you'd really have to reduce that 39% return by the interest rate you lost when you took the money out of the traditional bank to invest it.

Whatever you're financing, it works better through your Private Family Bank™.

NOTE: technically, the growth inside the policy is "tax-deferred," however, we show you how to access the money in your bank without tax consequences, so – for practical purposes – it is tax-free for you.

You're building 2 banks at the same time

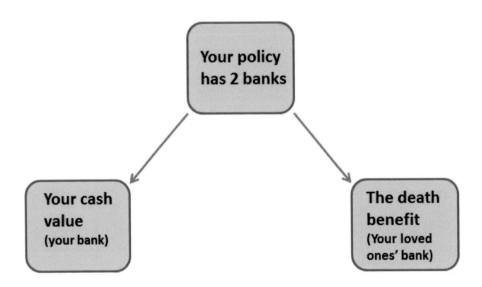

As you capitalize your Private Family Bank™, remember that it has 2 components: **your bank** (policy cash value), and **your loved ones' bank** (policy death benefit).

Your bank is money you can all use while you're still here. Your loved ones' bank is money for them when you're gone.

When you consider both banks as a return on your premium investment, there is no other investment or savings vehicle that even comes close to your Private Family Bank™.

The moment the policy takes effect, the insurance company immediately guarantees that your loved ones' bank is fully capitalized with an initial death benefit far above your initial premiums.

Over time, your premiums capitalize your bank – the policy's cash value. So, your bank grows, and your loved ones' bank grows along with it. Win-win!

Published by SMARTEST Wealth Systems – © Copyright 2017 • John Cummuta • all rights reserved

Chapter 4 – Let's build a wealth system

It should be clear by this point that we're not talking about life insurance as most people think of it. I should say, "...as most *less-than-wealthy* people think of it."

You see, the wealthy use life insurance this way all the time. They understand the incredible power of stacking returns like we just did in the previous investment example, and they really understand the power of having their wealth reside and grow, tax free, in one of the safest repositories on the planet – a whole life insurance policy.

When we use life insurance contracts the way the wealthy use them, we're building a living financing system instead of just a death benefit with a little savings component. Plus, we're building a bank for our loved ones, with a death benefit that ends up being effectively cost-free after a few years!

You'll get some of these benefits the moment you pay your first premium. Others take a while to build up, but then they become engines of wealth-creation: wealth residing safely in a tax favored account that is protected from lawsuits and judgments (varies by state).

From the moment your policy goes into effect, even if you've only paid one monthly premium, your family has the protection of the full initial death benefit. The insurance company immediately guarantees that amount in your loved ones' bank.

So, your estate has instantly grown by tens of thousands, hundreds of thousands, or more dollars! Unless you cancel or collapse the policy, a death benefit **will be paid** to your beneficiary(ies). It is not "maybe" money. That's why I call it your loved ones' bank.

You and they can bank on it.

Once you've built up your policy's cash value a bit, you can begin using it to finance your lifetime purchases the same way you've been using traditional banks.

Depending on the size of your premiums it may take a while to build up to where you can buy a car, but you can certainly pay off debts, finances less-expensive purchases, and have an emergency fund with much less in your bank.

Eventually, you'll be able to finance vacations, home remodels, and perhaps even your mortgage.

When used in a business, a Private Family Bank™ death benefit can fund a buy-sell agreement, while the cash value can provide a financing facility for growth and a repository for capital reserves.

Just build your bank, and then productively use it as soon as you can.

Build your wealth following the Wealth Pyramid

We'll start at the base of the pyramid on the next page.

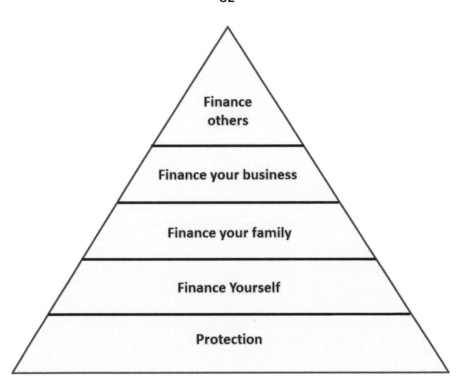

The first level of your Private Family Bank™ is protection, and as I said above, you get this level when you pay your first premium. Your loved ones are protected immediately. It provides security and peace.

Over time – depending on the size of your premiums – **you will soon be able to finance yourself**. If you have debts, this begins with paying off past purchases made with borrowed money. In other words, debt-elimination.

From there, you can grow to self-finance major purchases like furnishings, remodeling, vacations, cars, and other purchases with commas in the price. At this level, you want to repay these policy loans, because you want to always be planning to enjoy the maximum Available Loan Amount possible at retirement, or whatever you call your post-employment years.

When the "Finance Yourself" level is covered, **you can begin offering financing to family members**, usually children and grandchildren.

They need TVs, house down-payments, cars, educations, and so on. If they don't have great incomes, they will likely finance these purchases. Why not have them pay the interest to you?

I recommend that you treat these loans as LOANS, and you have family members sign promissory notes and commit to making the payments. You can, if you choose, give them some slack if they lose their income or have some other crisis, but if you treat these loans cavalierly, so will your borrowers.

Once your Private Family Bank™ is functioning as your financing source for your major purchases, and those of chosen family members, **you can consider using your bank's financing capability to start or grow a business of your own**.

Or you can be a lender to other people's businesses.

A business financing example

Here's an example of a business with some typical debts. There's a credit card balance, a business vehicle loan, some inventory that was financed, and a piece of business equipment with a loan. We'll say it's your business, but it could be someone else's.

Let's see how your Private Family Bank™ could help your business grow, and build your personal wealth at the same time.

Just like with Tom and Mary's car buying bank, you'll capitalize this bank at $10,000 a year over 4 years, but you'll start using it at the end of year 1.

The first year $6,000 is borrowed from your bank to pay off the credit card debt. The $500 monthly payment that was going to the credit card issuing bank is then redirected to the insurance company as loan repayment.

In year 2, you borrow $14,500 from your bank, which is possible because you paid another $10,000 premium, plus you paid back the $6,000 you borrowed to pay off the credit card. Once again, you redirect the former $500 car payment to the insurance company, so you are now paying them $1,000 a month loan repayment.

In year 3 you pay off $21,000 worth of inventory with a loan from your Private Family Bank™ made possible by that year's $10,000 premium plus $12,000 in repayments on the car and credit card loans.

Finally, in year 4, you borrow $31,100 to pay off your forklift. They money is there because of year four's $10,000 premium plus the $21,600 paid back on the credit card, car, and inventory loans.

- **At this point you have invested $40,000 in premiums, but have taken $72,600 out of your Private Family Bank™!**
- **The business' cash flow was not changed during this time, just redirected.**
- **And every dollar you've run through your bank is still in your bank earning interest and dividends!**

Lois and I have used our bank to finance repairs and improvements to rental homes we own. Our real estate LLC makes tax-deductible payments back to me and I make tax-deductible payments back to my Private Family Bank™.

The net result is that the interest payments made by our LLC reduce its profit, thereby reducing our taxes; and the whole time the money is growing in our **personal** Private Family Bank™, tax free. So, it's a win-win.

If you don't have a business of your own, you can use this exact process to lend money to someone who does. It's your bank. You decide who deserves to pay you interest!

Just make sure all the binding paperwork is in place.

Now let's make your wealth system *permanent*

So far, we've seen how your Private Family Bank™ can be used to finance your life, your family's lives, your business' life, other people's lives, and become a personal wealth-building system for you at the same time.

But what about the word "Permanent" in this book's title?

Well, your Private Family Bank™ wealth system can become permanent when you make it *generational* like Mayer Rothschild did.

Rothschild was born in 1744 in Frankfurt, Germany. He developed a family bank and spread his empire by installing each of his five sons in the five main European financial centers to conduct business.

The Rothschild coat of arms contains a clenched fist with 5 arrows symbolizing the 5 dynasties established by Rothschild's sons, in a reference to Psalm 127: "Like arrows in the hands of a warrior, so are the children of one's youth."

Mayer didn't just give his arrows – his sons – money when he passed on. He gave them a wealth system...a banking wealth system. You can do the same thing with Private Family Banks™.

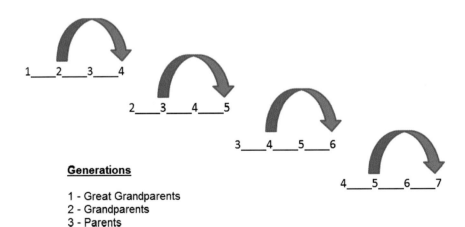

Generations

1 - Great Grandparents
2 - Grandparents
3 - Parents
4 - Children

In this system, the great grandparents (generation 1) are already living out their lives on the cash value in their Private Family Banks™.

The grandparents (generation 2), however, are creating their legacy by capitalizing banks for their grandchildren (generation 4). These banks can be used to provide student loans, car loans, or whatever might be useful and worthy. The important point is that the grandparents aren't just giving their grandkids money. They're giving them a wealth system.

The grandparent owns the policy and controls the bank, up to the point where they feel the grandchild is mature enough to run the bank him- or herself. At that point, ownership can be transferred to the grandchild. This way they get money (the policy's cash value) **and a system to multiply it**.

When generation 2 passes on, their bank is liquidated and the proceeds are passed to generation 3, who use the proceeds to build their own banks and to capitalize banks for generation 5.

When generation 3 passes on, their assets move to generation 4, who capitalize banks for generation 6, and so it continues, with the amounts growing with each succeeding generation. And the increase is mainly coming from the growing insurance company death benefits.

As each succeeding generation gets greater death benefit money from the preceding generation's policies, they can start larger Private Family Banks™ of their own...which will cascade even larger death benefits to their succeeding generation.

It worked pretty well for the Rothschilds. Their family wealth is now estimated at between $1 and $100 Trillion! No one knows for sure because their wealth is private and global.

Chapter 5 – Why wouldn't I do this?

About this time, your inner voice should be asking this question. I mean…

- You get a platform that will grow your money at the same time you use it to pay off your debts, if you have any.
- You get a savings vehicle that's arguably safer than a bank savings account or CD, and pays a much higher return than banks or government bonds.
- You get an investing platform that allows you to continue earning that higher return on money you take out of your bank to place in investments, along with the return from those investments.
- You get hassle-free self-financing of the things you need and want
- You get an immediate and dramatic increase in your family net worth (death benefit – your loved ones' bank)
- And once you put money in your bank, it should be **forever tax free** to you and your heirs.

However, some of us encounter subconscious and even conscious roadblocks, because of our traditional view of whole life insurance. So, let me deal with those.

It's "death insurance"

You may view life insurance as "Death" insurance. My father sure did. I can remember him saying, "I hate paying for something where I have to die to win!"

Dad was looking at life insurance as death insurance, and since he was talking about term insurance, he was right. He saw it as a *cost* in *his* life so there could be a later *gain* in *our* lives once he was gone.

He would pay for it, but he wouldn't enjoy any benefits from it himself.

However, that is not what we're talking about here. We are using a whole life insurance contract, which automatically builds a cash account within the policy, and we're souping it up so it builds cash even faster for you.

It is life insurance, but in our application, the death benefit is not its primary function. We are designing the policy to maximize its wealth-growing and financing capabilities, and – in most applications – we view the death benefit as an important but secondary bonus.

A Private Family Bank™ is a living financial system, with one component that builds wealth that you and your loved ones can use and enjoy together, while you're alive.

When you pass on, the second bank component provides money for those you leave behind.

So, you don't have to feel guilty about spending the money in your cash value during your post-employment years, because **the insurance company is standing there with a pile of money that you did not have to earn or save up.** And they promise to give that money to your loved ones when you're no longer there to provide it for them.

Published by SMARTEST Wealth Systems – © Copyright 2017 • John Cummuta • all rights reserved

Your financial advisors

Your insurance agent and accountant have likely never learned about modifying a participating whole life insurance policy to function as a **living financial system** rather than as death insurance. So, don't be surprised if they give you a funny look or even disparage the idea, if you mention it to them.

The insurance and accounting professions are complicated enough in their normal course of business without turning one of their familiar boxes inside out. So, if you've never heard of this concept from your insurance and tax advisors, it's probably because they've never heard of it either.

Of course, hundreds of thousands of these policies are already in effect, so the secret is getting out.

It hits them in the pocketbook

If I engineer a Private Family Bank™ policy for you, I'll be intentionally reducing my commission by 50% to 70%, compared to what I would earn if I sold you the exact same whole life policy with the same premium amount, but without the modifications that supercharge its performance as a banking platform.

The internal policy modifications we make to feed more of your premiums dollars directly into your cash value, take most of that money from our potential sales commission. We're literally sending more than half our commission into your first-year bank deposit.

I'm not looking for sympathy here. I and my Private Family Banking™ associates are willing to take that cut, because we're that committed to giving you a tool that can help you win the game. Our mission has always been to provide education and services to help our hard-working, fellow middle-class Americans get to a better financial outcome than they will by default.

Plus, we get a lot more referrals and additional policy sales than traditional insurance agents, because what we're offering performs better for the client than for the agent.

Most other financial professionals have good intentions for their clients, but they're stuck in a "we've always done it this way" box, offering the same old products for the same old reasons.

Most life insurance agents, for example, either don't know about this application of whole life insurance or don't want to cut their income in half or more. So, the idea is dead on arrival for them.

As for accountants and tax preparers, consider whether they would like a major part of your financial world to become "tax free" for you. As an industry, they need things to be taxable, deductible, and complicated, so they can manipulate the numbers to "save you money."

"I don't have the extra money"

Another emotional roadblock may be that you're struggling to think of where you'd get the "extra" money to do this. Well, it doesn't have to be extra.

The first phase of operating your Private Family Bank™ is using it as a savings account, so look for money you're already saving.

Are you currently funding a qualified retirement account, savings account, CD, or similar vehicle? Think about redirecting that money stream into premium to capitalize your Private Family Bank™.

Are you overpaying any debt payments to accelerate their payoff? Consider redirecting that overpayment money into your banking policy's premiums.

These are money streams that are already going toward improving your future finances, so redirecting them to your Private Family Bank™ won't impact your daily lifestyle or cash flow.

Of course, we can all become a bit more disciplined about where our money goes in a typical month.

My experience has been that most people have a lot of monthly cash flow just leaking out of their lives in the form of periodic indulgences. Many of these expenditures won't stand up to scrutiny, so scrutinize them to see if they really are more important to you than achieving financial independence is.

Use the *Premium Finder Form* in the appendix of this book to help you locate leaking money.

As I mentioned earlier, another quick tool to help find unnecessary expenditures is my CIA acronym.

No, it's not about spies or the government. CIA stands for **C**onvenience, **I**ndulgence, and **A**ppearance. These three areas are the biggest money-wasters in most people lives. Watch out for them.

I'm not sure I'd pass the physical

We are talking about life insurance, so the physical condition of the insured is a factor. Let's look at that.

The medical requirements for an insurance company to approve a policy application are probably not as strict as you might think, but there are standards.

Insurance companies employ people to determine the risk of insuring a person's life. These underwriters, as they're called, look at the information provided on the application, they check a national medical database called the Medical Information Bureau, they may request medical records from the proposed insured's physician, and they will likely – at insurance company expense – have a paramedic or doctor give the proposed insured an in-home medical exam.

Based on this information, the underwriter may conclude the proposed insured is a better than average risk, and thereby offer them *preferred* status, which would produce a higher death benefit and a somewhat faster cash value build for the same premium.

Most people, even many on medications, are evaluated to be *standard* risks and are offered a standard rated policy. This is the average for most people, and the Standard requirements "bake in" many of the medical realities and medications of aging.

Some people, based on their medical history, are found to be *substandard* risks, and they are offered what's often called a "rated policy," meaning its numbers are based on a numeric rate table lower than Standard. This generally results in a reduced death benefit and somewhat slower cash value growth.

The 4th category includes those people who are determined to be too high a risk for the insurance company, and they are declined.

Being declined would be the end of the process…if the goal was primarily to get a death benefit on your life. But if we're talking about building a Private Family Bank™ that you own and control, being declined is not the end.

Here's why not.

In addition to the insurance company, there are 3 parties to a life insurance contract: the policy owner, the insured, and the beneficiary. The policy owner and the insured life are most often the same person, but they do not have to be.

The owner of the policy pays the premiums, controls the cash value, and can establish and change beneficiaries. It's their bank. The "insured" is the person on whose life the insurance company is taking the risk. It would be their death that would trigger payment of the death benefit.

A potential policy owner can take out a policy on their own life, where they would be both policy owner and insured, or they can take out a policy on the life of anyone in whom they have an "insurable interest." They would be the owner and controller of the bank within the policy, but theirs would not be the life the policy insures.

According to the Society of Actuaries, there 2 ways to have an insurable interest in the context of a life insurance policy:

- An interest based upon a reasonable expectation of pecuniary (financial) advantage through the continued life, health and bodily safety of another person, and,

Published by SMARTEST Wealth Systems – © Copyright 2017 • John Cummuta • all rights reserved

consequently, loss by reason of their death or disability. This can include the life of an income provider to a household, a business partner, or a key employee in a business.

- A substantial interest engendered by love and affection, if closely related by blood or by law.

What this means, in the context of building a Private Family Bank™, is that, if your health doesn't pass the muster for insuring your own life, you can take out a policy – which you own and control – that insures the life of someone in which you have an insurable interest. That could be anyone from a spouse, to a child, to a business partner or key employee.

OK, there's one more potential tripping hazard on your way to your own Private Family Bank™. Maybe your subconscious has the objection that you were taught to…

"Buy term and invest the difference"

Popularized by A.L. Williams in the 1970's, the fact that you can buy more death benefit per premium dollar with term insurance became a mantra to a generation of financial advisors and insurance agents.

It seemed to make so much sense. Why not buy $150,000 worth of term insurance for a similar premium to what would only buy $15,000 worth of whole life insurance?

But this simple comparison doesn't tell the whole story. Let's look at it a different way. We'll compare two $500,000 policies: one an unmodified, basic, off-the-shelf whole life contract, the other a term policy.

We'll start with the difference in purpose between the 2 types of policies.

Whole life is insurance for your *whole life*...until you die...so it's designed by the insurance company with the knowledge that it is much more likely to be held until the death benefit is paid to a beneficiary.

Term insurance, on the other hand, is designed to be used for a period of time – a term – but not all the way to death. So, it's much less likely that a death benefit will be paid.

In fact, **less than 2% of term life insurance policies ever pay a death benefit.**

The main reason for this is that term insurance premiums get larger as the insured ages, because they are getting closer to death and therefore present a greater risk to the insurance company. At some point premiums become unsustainably expensive, and the policy is dropped.

Sometime later, the person dies, uninsured, after having paid the term insurance company thousands of premium dollars over their lifetime.

A fundamental difference with whole life is that, while some of your premium is going to pay for the death benefit, a significant portion is simultaneously going to build your cash value, which is your money to use as you see fit.

A term insurance premium is just renting a death benefit that the insurance company is 98% sure you'll never claim. No cash builds for you in a term policy. No equity of any kind is building for you.

Published by SMARTEST Wealth Systems – © Copyright 2017 • John Cummuta • all rights reserved

My dad was right about term insurance: "You have to die to win."

OK, let's get to the numbers to see how significant these differences turn out to be. We'll go across the rows in the below table.

It certainly starts out looking like term insurance is the clear winner. In this example, you'll pay nearly $8,000 in annual premiums for a $500,000 whole life policy, but under $1,000 for the same half-million-dollar death benefit in a term policy.

Since the term policy is for a term of time – 20 years in this case – we'll use that time frame for our comparison.

Policy parameters	Basic Whole Life insurance	20 year Term Life insurance
Premium paid per year	$7,970	$980
Total premiums after 20 yrs.	$159,400	$19,600
Policy cash value	$179,920	$0
Death benefit age 65 (20yr)	$537,556	$500,000
Death benefit age 66	$537,556	$0

Moving down to the next row we see that, over the 2 decades we'll pay almost $160,000 in whole life premiums but less than $20,000 in term premiums. Term wins again.

But wait!

Drop down to the next row and we find that our whole life policy has built up nearly $180,000 in cash value, whereas the term policy has accumulated $0. We paid $160,000 in premiums, and our whole life policy has generated $20,000 in profits, which is more than the term policy costs over 20 years,

So – in effect – the death benefit was free in the whole life policy. It was paid for by the interest and dividends generated inside the account.

Go down another line and we find that, not only has the cash built up inside the whole life policy, but the death benefit has grown as well. This is another $37,556 advantage over the term policy.

Finally, the bottom row shows that the day after the end of the term policy's 20th year (66th birthday in this example), the whole life policy is still guaranteeing a $537,556 death benefit, but the term policy death benefit has evaporated.

Of course, the term insurance buyer could go back to their insurance company and ask for a new term policy to start up at age 66, but the premium could be over $20,000 a year! That's more in 1 year than the expiring term policy cost for 2 decades.

Why?

Because at age 66 the insured is much closer to death, so the number of years the insurance company is likely to be able to collect premiums is fewer than the 20 years of the previous term. Plus, the insurance company knows that anyone willing to pay these expensive premiums is likely concerned about their physical insurability, and is therefore likely to keep the policy until it pays a death benefit, increasing the risk for the insurance company.

Remember, this comparison is between a term policy and a *standard, cookie-cutter, unmodified whole life policy.*

By comparison, a whole life contract specifically engineered to be a Private Family Bank™ would generate greater cash value build-up.

The above table was simply to show that even a standard whole life policy provides much greater overall value than a term policy over time.

But what about the "invest the difference" part?

The value claim of "Buy term and invest the difference" is based on actually investing the difference. The fact is that most people don't invest the difference. They spend the difference.

Plus, even if they do invest the difference, what do they invest it in? They'll probably put it in the stock market. I hope I've shown how undependable that can be.

Just ask yourself, would you likely invest the difference with consistency? And, if you would invest the difference, where would you likely invest it? Would it go into mutual funds that invest in stocks?

If you had invested $10,000 in the U.S. stock market (S&P 500) in the first week of January 2003, by the first week of January 2013 it would've been worth $15,810; but that $5,810 gain is taxable. At the 20% capital gains tax rate (just counting federal) that gain would be reduced to $4,648, so you'd have $14,648 after taxes.

On the other hand, **$10,000 in your Private Family Bank™ cash value over those 10 years would have grown to $15,208...and it would be protected from taxes.**

Your Private Family Bank™ would have outperformed the stock market by $560, and that's if you had left the money in the stock market during the whole decade.

Note: the interest rate paid inside your Private Family Bank™ trends with market interest rates, so if inflation comes back, the money in your bank will progressively earn higher interest.

Summary

The advantages of building your own Private Family Bank™ include:

- You establish **a regular savings regime** that gently forces you to be a more consistent saver than you would likely be on your own.
- You can enjoy **wealth-building gains** that rival the average mutual fund investor's stock market return, **with dramatically reduced risk.**
- You can **pay off** your cars, home, student loans, credit cards, and other debts while simultaneously building retirement wealth...**using the same dollars.**
- You realize **an immediate gain** to the estate you will pass on to your loved ones (policy death benefit). I call this your loved ones' bank.
- You can **build your wealth tax free.**
- You can **use your wealth tax free.**
- You can **recover the 34.5%,** or whatever your percentage is, of your after-tax income that you're losing to interest costs.
- You can enjoy the growth of all that **recaptured interest earning interest** itself.
- You can **reduce your taxes** and your heirs' taxes.
- You can **eliminate contribution and withdrawal restrictions** of qualified retirement plans.
- You can **enjoy unrestricted liquidity, control, and use** of your money for any reason.

- You can **protect your wealth** from creditors, judgments, and law suits. (varies by state)
- You can be assured **your wealth plan would succeed** even if you are disabled.
- You can be assured **your wealth plan would succeed** even if you die before you complete it.
- You can **pass your wealth on** to your heirs **tax free**.

Now, let's summarize what you will <u>lose</u> if you don't start your own Private Family Bank™:

- You **won't likely** establish **a regular savings regime** that forces you to be more consistent than you would likely be on your own.
- You won't enjoy **wealth-building gains** that rival the average mutual fund investor's stock market return, **and you'll undertake dramatically higher risks.**
- You **won't pay off** your cars, home, student loans, credit cards, and other debts while simultaneously building retirement wealth...**using the same dollars**.
- You **won't** realize **an immediate gain** to the estate you will pass on to your loved ones.
- You **won't build your wealth tax free**.
- You **won't** be able to **use your wealth tax free**.
- You **won't recover the 34.5%,** or whatever your percentage is, of your after-tax income that you're losing to interest costs.
- You **won't** enjoy all that **recaptured interest earning interest** itself.
- You **won't reduce your taxes** and your heirs' taxes.

Published by SMARTEST Wealth Systems – © Copyright 2017 • John Cummuta • all rights reserved

- You **won't eliminate contribution and withdrawal restrictions** of qualified retirement plans.
- You **won't enjoy unrestricted liquidity, control, and use** of your money for any reason.
- You **won't protect your wealth** from creditors, judgments, and law suits.
- You **won't** be assured **your wealth plan would succeed** even you are disabled.
- You **won't** be assured **your wealth plan would succeed** even if you die before you complete it.
- You **won't** likely **pass all your wealth on** to your heirs **tax free**.

Your current investment choices are:

- Bank savings, money market, or interest checking account ≈½% 1%
- CD ≈ 1% 2%
- U.S. Treasury notes and bonds: 1 yr. ≈ .83%, 5 yr. ≈ .1.93%, 10 yr. ≈ 2.48%
- Stock Market ≈ 5.19% (over 20 years, according to research firm Dalbar, Inc.)

If you're still not convinced you should have a Private Family Bank™, there's nothing more I can say to move the dial. If you're willing to end up with less, and expose what you do end up with to market risks and federal/state taxes, I have nothing to offer you...except to share the immortal words of Sponge Bob Square Pants: "Good luck with that."

If, on the other hand, you're as uncomfortable with the last couple decades as I am, we need to talk.

If you're as queasy about the next couple decades as I am, we definitely need to talk. Why?

Have you had enough of this?

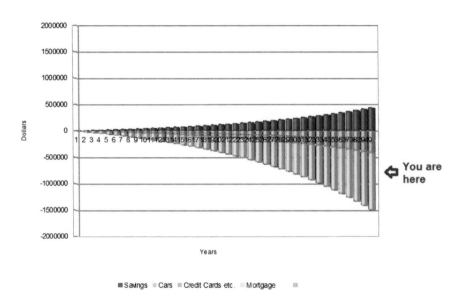

Are you ready to start this?

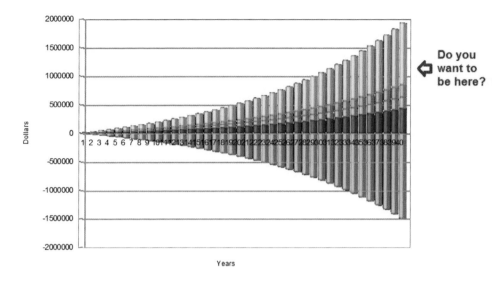

That's what I thought.

How do you get started?

The first thing you must do at this point is to remind yourself of your *why*.

If you recall in the Introduction to this book I explained your *why* as the answer to the question, "*Why* would I undertake the disciplines necessary to achieve this or any other financial game plan?"

Your *why* is your overarching, gut-level, emotional purpose for making and saving more money, both in the short and long term. So, what are the factors that make up your *why*?

If you're like most people, your *why* is actually a *who*, or a number of *who's*. Your *why* is likely based on your desire to build financial security and peace of mind for those you care about most, including yourself.

As you think about the 2 banks a Private Family Bank™ policy would create – the cash value for you and your loved ones to use now and the death benefit for your loved ones' needs later – try to feel what providing these banks would mean to you and them.

That feeling is your *why*.

Once you're in touch with your *why*, there may still be questions about how a policy can be designed for your unique circumstances. I and my team will be happy to have that no-cost, no-obligation discussion with you and answer those questions.

Just call 602-527-3969 or email info@smartestwealthsystems.com to get the conversation started.

Published by SMARTEST Wealth Systems – © Copyright 2017 • John Cummuta • all rights reserved

We'll customize a policy to maximize your money's:

- Guaranteed growth
- Tax-free growth
- Liquidity
- Safety
- Control
- Privacy
- Self-financing capability
- Protection from taxes
- Protection from judgments (lawsuits)
- Tax-free distribution to your beneficiaries

We'll coach you on how to:

- Find the money to capitalize your bank.
- Grow your Private Family Bank™
- **Use your bank.**
- **Our online and live trainings cover subjects like:**
  - Buying cars and making other purchases through your bank
  - Paying off your debts
  - Investing through your bank
  - Funding vacations
  - Funding college
  - Funding your business
  - Building a generational system of PFBs

PS – if you're an insurance agent (or would like to be) and would like to join our team, just email your interest to agent@smartestwealthsystems.com.

Appendix

PFB Premium Finder Form

STEP ONE: Total Household Income

Income Source	Earner A	Earner B
Salary (net, take-home pay)	$	$
Part-time or self-employment income	$	$
Home-based business income	$	$
Investment Income	$	$
Social Security	$	$
Pension	$	$
Veteran's Benefits	$	$
Other	$	$
Individual totals:	$	$
Total Income Earner A + Earner B =	$	

STEP TWO: Reducing Your Monthly Expenses.

List all your current monthly expenses in the **Current** column below. In the **Reduced** column write in the lowest amount you can reasonably spend on each expense item.

Total up all **Reduced** amounts at the bottom of column 3, then subtract that amount from your **Total Income** above. The resulting number is your maximum possible starting Private Family Bank™ Premium.

If you feel you need to use a lower Premium amount to give yourself some breathing room each month, that's your decision. It will just take you a little longer to capitalize your Private Family Bank™.

Monthly Expenses	Current	Reduced
Retirement plan contributions		
Other savings		
Going out for lunch at work		
Dining out (other than work lunches)		
Groceries		
Telephone (including cell)		

Heating fuel		
Water/Sewer		
Electricity		
Car costs (fuel and maintenance)		
Parking, tolls, etc.		
Car #1 payment		
Car #2 payment		
Insurance – Automobile		
Insurance – Health		
Insurance – Home		
Insurance – Life		
Insurance – Other		
Home equity loan payment		
Other loan payment		
Child care		
Cable or Satellite TV		

Movies out and video rentals		
Other entertainment		
Sports (golf, fishing, etc.)		
Health Club		
Lawn Maintenance		
Laundry		
Pet food and care		
Subscriptions		
Online computer services		
Credit card payment		
Credit card payment		
Credit card payment		
Total Reduced Monthly Expenses =		
Total Income – Total Reduced Monthly Expenses = Your Available Premium ➡		

Private Family Banking™
Policy Customization Questions

Name of Insured: _____

Name of Policy Owner: _____

Best Phone #: _____

Email Address: _____

Insured's birthdate: _____ Insured's Gender: M / F

Insured's Health: □ Generally good   □ Some issues   □ Challenged

Medical conditions and meds:

_____

_____

What's your #1 short-term financial goal? _____

_____

What's your #1 long-term financial goal? _____

_____

What's your greatest financial concern? _____

_____

How much money (monthly/quarterly/annually) do you feel comfortable committing to the program? $_____/_____ (see accompanying Premium Finder Form)

Do you have any amounts already in other accounts or life insurance policies you could transfer to your PFB policy to help capitalize it? You'd essentially be repositioning it from an existing account you own to a new account you own. $_____

The Application Process:

- We will design one or more proposed policy illustrations for you, and then set up an appointment to review them with you.
- Once you've selected the policy design you like best, we will take your application (about a half hour), and then call to schedule the in-home medical exam. (no cost to you)
- The insurance company underwriters will gather any additional info they need, such as records from your doctor.
- If all is well (it almost always is), the underwriters will offer you the policy.
- You will then pay your first premium (the first time any money comes from you).
- The whole process takes 3-4 weeks in most cases.

To talk to me, my partner Tony Manganiello, or one of our licensed and trained associates:

602-527-3969
info@smartestwealthsystems.com

Disclaimer

None of Content and Design, Inc dba SMARTEST Wealth Systems, its
owners (expressly including but not limited to John M. Cummuta and
Anthony Manganiello), officers, directors, employees, subsidiaries,
affiliates, licensors, service providers, content providers and agents (all
collectively hereinafter referred to as the "Publisher") are financial
educators and nothing contained herein is intended to be or to be
construed as financial advice.

"Content and Design is not an investment advisory service, is not an
investment adviser, and does not provide personalized financial advice or
act as a financial adviser.

The Banker's Secret to Permanent Family Wealth™ exists for educational
purposes only, and the materials and information contained herein are for
general informational purposes only. None of the information provided in
the book or associated videos is intended as investment, tax, accounting, or
legal advice. The information in the materials should not be solely relied
upon for purposes of transacting any investment or purchase.

The reader hereby understands and agrees that *The Banker's Secret to
Permanent Family Wealth™* and Content and Design, Inc. do not offer or
provide tax, legal or investment advice and that you are responsible for
consulting tax, legal, or financial professionals before acting on any
information provided herein.

Your use of the information contained herein is at your own risk. The
content is provided 'as is' and without warranties of any kind, either
expressed or implied. Content and Design, Inc. disclaims all warranties,
including, but not limited to, any implied warranties of merchantability,
fitness for a particular purpose, title, or non-infringement. Content and
Design, Inc. does not promise or guarantee any income or particular result
from your use of the information contained herein. Content and Design,

Inc. assumes no liability or responsibility for errors or omissions in the information contained herein.

Content and Design, Inc. will not be liable for any incidental, direct, indirect, punitive, actual, consequential, special, exemplary, or other damages, including, but not limited to, loss of revenue or income, pain and suffering, emotional distress, or similar damages, even if Content and Design, Inc. has been advised of the possibility of such damages. In no event, will the collective liability of Content and Design, Inc. to any party (regardless of the form of action, whether in contract, tort, or otherwise) exceed the greater of $100 or the amount you have paid to Content and Design, Inc. for the information, product, or service out of which liability arose.

Under no circumstances will Content and Design, Inc. be liable for any loss or damage caused by your reliance on the information contained herein. It is your responsibility to evaluate the accuracy, completeness or usefulness of any information, opinion, advice, or other content contained herein. Please seek the advice of professionals, as appropriate, regarding the evaluation of any specific information, opinion, advice, or other content.

Printed in Great Britain
by Amazon